themoodbook

themoodbook

identify and explore 100 moods and emotions

andrea harrn

Eddison Books Ltd

This edition published in Great Britain in 2019
by Eddison Books Limited
www.eddisonbooks.com

Text and illustrations copyright © Andrea Harrn 2019
This edition copyright © Eddison Books Limited 2019

Illustrations by Stacey Siddons

British Library Cataloguing-in-Publication data available on request.

ISBN 978-1-85906-428-3

1 3 5 7 9 10 8 6 4 2

Printed in Europe

CONTENTS

Introduction

This book explores the highs and lows, the complexities and intensities, as well as the positively joyous pleasures and successes, of 21st-century life. It's a collection of moods, emotions, feelings, states of mind and quirks of personality, and includes some mood disorders, as well as some common personality types and characteristics.

This is a book for people who are interested in learning more about how and why they feel the way they do. Each page includes a concise definition of the mood or emotion, along with common signs and/or symptoms to help with identification, followed by examples and anecdotes to interpret and make sense of things that can often be confusing and overwhelming. A section on support and guidance gives solid practical ideas and inspiration for moving forward, while the questions posed prompt you to think about your personal experience and how you might be able to take steps to make positive changes. Reading through the pages will not only help you to understand yourself but will also challenge your thinking – which can be life-changing. The examples given at the back of the book can help you relate the scenarios to your own life and to those around you, offering insight into how moods and emotions may play a role in a variety of situations, within relationships and both work and family settings.

As a psychotherapist with almost twenty years' experience, I have included many issues, problems and dilemmas that present to me in my therapy room on a regular basis. This can range from stress and depression to addictive behaviours, abuse, relationship issues, low self-esteem, confidence or grief. I use an integrative approach in my therapy practice, ranging from person-centred/humanistic to a more structured cognitive behavioural therapy (CBT) model. I integrate many ancient wisdoms from Eastern religion and philosophy – such as mindfulness and meditation – with positive psychology, neuro-linguistic programming (NLP) and hypnotherapy, all bound in an overall space of love and acceptance (the key components for human growth and development).

There are huge benefits to becoming emotionally intelligent, such as increased self-awareness, empathy, compassion and acceptance. Using the information in this book, you will gain fresh perspectives on situations and new ideas on how to respond and cope in different ways.

Our emotions are our guides, our intuitive wisdom, and it is vital that we pay attention to them. However, we also need to be grounded in reality. This book brings together spirituality and earthly experiences, to help you consider the right decisions for yourself.

How this book can help

There are many theories of emotions, dating back to Aristotle, who identified fourteen main ones: anger, mildness, love, enmity (hatred), fear, confidence, shame, shamelessness, benevolence, pity, indignation, envy, emulations and contempt. Since then, other philosophers, scientists and psychologists have grouped emotions into categories of basic/primary emotions, such as love, joy, surprise, anger, sadness, fear and disgust, with second and third levels of emotions that fall within those groups.

This book doesn't aim to classify emotions themselves, but more to give concrete examples of what it means to *feel* a certain way. Rather than putting things into boxes, it aims to open the boxes up and make links that are believable, credible and workable.

Furthermore, this book is not exhaustive. How many emotions are there anyway? There are also many other interpretations and examples that might have been given. There are so many different factors involved in human psychology and numerous ways to describe and verbalize feelings, with literally hundreds of words and combinations of language to choose from. Neither is this book a scientific study of why we have emotions in the first place; there is little mention of neuroscience or biology. This is not because this is not relevant or important. It is because my aim, as a psychotherapist, has always been to get to the root of the problem, and find creative solutions.

Moods and emotions are subjective and can be complex experiences, yet they can also be fleeting and simple. We all experience a variety of feelings every single day – positive and negative – which can relate to current experiences (such as the weather or a train being delayed) to finding out you've just been promoted at work. Our moods, emotions, thoughts and feelings relate to ourselves, others, conversations and past or future situations. They are the foundation of what makes up human experience.

Throughout our lives there will be ups and downs, which can be caused by our own actions, the actions of others or events out of our control, such as environmental issues or war. It is not so much a situation itself that causes disturbance within us, but more our interpretation of it. Thoughts are powerful, and assumptions more so. Feelings can be triggered in an instant, and this can set off a whole chain of unhelpful thinking and behaviours.

Some people are more able to manage their emotions than others, by recognition and acceptance. Others, such as those with mood disorders like bipolar or borderline personality disorder (BPD), struggle to make sense of themselves, which can cause all sorts of difficulties. When you have a bad feeling about a situation, is that a sign from within (your intuition) that you should avoid something, or is it based on a previous bad experience that is being triggered?

Primary inherent emotions are with us from birth and develop as we grow. Babies naturally feel love. They don't know it on a cognitive level – it's more of a felt experience. Children feel joy when they are contented and safe, or frustration when they can't express themselves or things don't go their way. The person we grow up to be is hugely influenced by early experience and modelling. What we see around us – our environment, our nurturing – creates our norm. Anxious parents are more likely to produce anxious children. Where children are not free to express their thoughts and feelings, they learn to hold on to them and, in an effort to please, will develop a false sense of self. When parents do not themselves have emotional stability, this creates an unsafe world for a child to grow in, and that sense of insecurity can be long-lasting. Children of parents with addictions can also feel abandoned, rejected and worthless, which ties in with shame and low self-esteem.

When a child grows up in a nurturing, loving environment, they feel secure. If they are given freedom to explore, be creative and make mistakes, they develop belief and confidence in themselves to try new things, knowing that they will not be rejected. This is unconditional love – the ideal environment for healthy emotional, physical and spiritual development.

This is no straightforward topic. It is multi-layered and multi-faceted. There will be many links between current emotional states and past experiences, and joining the dots can be both enlightening and empowering.

Why is it that some people are more emotional or sensitive than others? This can be a result of early experience, but also connects to personality type and right- versus left-brain thinking. People who are more connected to their left brain are naturally more logical, academic, analytical, rational and objective, whereas right-brainers are more intuitive, creative, subjective, random and emotional. It's very common for partners to choose someone quite opposite to themselves; what is lacking in you can be found in your partner. It can, however, be upsetting and frustrating when your partner doesn't 'get' you.

The emotional/physical connection

So, do our emotions occur as a result of physiological reaction to events, or does our physiology react as a result of our emotions? There are arguments on both sides. There are situations that happen where you feel out of control, such as grief or abuse, where you can feel knocked sideways. Emotions are so varied and complex and deeply personal. They can be confusing, mixed up and hard to pin down. There is *no* right or wrong way to feel in life. No judgement should be made on you, or by you.

There is a strong link between emotional well-being and physical health. The two cannot be separated. When people are anxious or depressed, this can lead to physical symptoms such as pain, insomnia, irritable bowel syndrome and even cancer. Our internal organs are a reflection of our state of mind. Physical exercise can have a profound impact on health and is widely known to reduce stress and depression, while meditation can help to slow breathing and quiet the mind. Mindfulness helps bring calm and acceptance to situations, and regular practice can improve relaxation, memory, empathy and self-esteem.

When we feel positive and calm, this relaxes our DNA and our neural path-ways. Conversely, when we feel negative, our bodies become tight and stressed. A calm and happy you can shine and radiate positive vibes, thereby helping others to feel calm. Your energy affects the world around you. Whether you are a parent, partner or employer, try to be the best you can be, so that others are able to benefit too.

There is no situation in life that cannot be mastered. Be accepting of yourself and others. Let go of what no longer serves you. Focus on where you want your life to go. Visualize your dreams. Be ready to embrace change. Believe in yourself, because *you* are capable of great things.

Ways to use the book

This book can be used as a reference guide, a self-help tool, or by parents and professionals (life coaches, therapists, counsellors, care workers, mental health professionals …), either on a one-to-one basis or in a group setting.

Try choosing a mood to explore at random – just open the book and see where the page takes you. Or, to address specific moods, emotions or behaviours, refer to the A–Z listing at the back of the book (see page 130). Alternatively, flick through the book to see if there are any facial expressions you are especially drawn to; this may indicate areas that it would be useful for you to explore at this time.

Some moods and emotions will be well known, and others less known; all will be enlightening, and will help you to learn more about yourself.

With this book you can:

- *Expand your knowledge of moods and emotions*
- *Discover definitions and meanings – some will be familiar and others will make you think in more depth*
- *Learn to recognize symptoms that you, or others close to you, may be experiencing*
- *Bring a common-sense approach to life difficulties*
- *Make sense of your own life*
- *Increase your self-awareness*
- *Expand your empathy*

- *Identify your own obstacles*
- *Gain ideas for moving forward*
- *Find your passion and reach your potential*

The case studies at the back of the book will help you to learn more about family dynamics, relationships, work situations, eating disorders, stress, anxiety, personal development, and so much more.

It is my pleasure to be able to share my thoughts, ideas, ramblings and experiences with you, and my hope is that you enjoy learning more about yourself.

May your dreams become realities.

Much love and peace to you all

Andrea

The moods and emotions

LONELY

I feel so alone.

Definition

Feeling alone, without anyone special, friends or company; feeling disconnected from others and from life itself; not having anyone to share your day, week or plans with. You can be in a big crowd and still feel alone.

Signs & symptoms

Feeling sad, confused, self-critical, isolated, needy, anxious.

There are two types of loneliness: social and emotional. These days, cities become transient bases and we don't always have time to get to know those around us. Emotional loneliness occurs when people feel alone with their concerns, which can happen even within a family or social group. The problem arises when people feel both social and emotional loneliness, which can lead to mental health issues such as stress or depression. Major life changes can also contribute to feeling isolated, such as having a baby, becoming a carer or retiring. A bereavement or break-up – where life has changed drastically, perhaps through no fault of our own – can leave us feeling lost in our thoughts and feelings. Friends and family may try to support you, but when they leave it's just you, with only your loneliness for company.

Support & guidance There are things we can all do to help ourselves feel less isolated. We're all part of a wider network of humanity, not alone in this world – although it may feel that way. If you're expecting others to lift you out of your loneliness, you may be waiting a long time. It's really down to you. Try to do more, take time for conversations – even with passing strangers. Give people in your life a chance to connect with you on an emotional level. If you struggle to socialize, come out of your comfort zone, join a group or start a new hobby to stimulate your mind and re-energize yourself. Say yes to invites. Remember: wherever there is a human being, there is an opportunity for kindness and connection, and, although it may be hard to walk alone, every step you take may be the start of a new friendship.

How would you like your life to be?
What can you do to help yourself feel more connected?

SENSITIVE

Definition

Hypersensitive to others; heightened emotional reactions to subtle or more obvious energies.

Signs & symptoms

Being empathic and sympathetic; sometimes feeling emotionally overwhelmed by others; being a psychic or a healer.

Are you a sensitive soul? Being sensitive can be a blessing and a burden. Sensitive people pick up on others' moods, emotions, thoughts and actions in a way that touches, prods, hits and can momentarily destabilize. A sensitive person can feel weak and undefended when faced with the unexpected. It might be an unkind word or a criticism. It could be someone else's trauma that lands in your lap, or it might be picking up on something that is about to implode or explode. Sensitive types can also be psychic, clairvoyant or clairsentient; being sensitive is part of their soul, DNA, personality and life. Alternatively, if you think others are too sensitive, it can stop you from being honest in your communication.

Support & guidance We can work on our sensitivities by learning how to protect ourselves from negative energies. When you know someone is likely to raise your emotions in an unhelpful way, try to be guarded around them. Put an energetic boundary around yourself by grounding yourself and then strengthening your aura, surrounding it in white or golden light. Be assertive about what is and isn't possible. This may be hard to do, as sensitive people are often the listeners and healers, used to putting others first. Having sensitivity overload can weaken you, so don't allow yourself to become drained by others. Being able to support others by empathizing deeply with them is a blessing, but it's imperative that you take care of yourself first, to stay healthy, energized, positive and whole. Being sensitive doesn't make you weak, just a little fragile sometimes.

How does being sensitive affect your life?
What do you do to protect yourself from being overwhelmed by others?

ADHD

Definition

Having a unique way of thinking and seeing the world; diagnosed as a disorder because it is outside the 'norm'. Involves inattentiveness and hyperactivity.

Signs & symptoms

Being easily distracted, impatient, restless and forgetful.

In childhood, this is the kid who can't sit still, concentrate or carry out instructions. It's the little chatterbox who forgets things and loses things. Being told off by teachers and parents can lead to feelings of low self-worth, where the child feels different, naughty. They are quite probably impulsive, compulsive and obsessive, can't wait their turn, act and speak without thinking, and have little sense of danger. Too many children are given medication to control their behaviour rather than being encouraged to be themselves. Some people with ADHD find relationships difficult, because their social cues and way they understand the world is different to others'. Being 'all over the place' may be fine for you, but not necessarily for everyone. It can cause disruption, discontent and frustration. It's not easy being different.

Support & guidance Having ADHD as an adult can be both an awesome and a challenging experience. There is no longer anyone to say, 'No, sit down, do as you're told.' The sky is the limit and the choices are endless. You don't fit into a box, but why be stuck in a box? There is so much more to the world than a set of rules and expectations. Thinking differently allows you great opportunity to be imaginative and innovative. Many successful entrepreneurs, thought leaders and business experts have ADHD. To be creative and successful doesn't require staying power; it just needs self-acceptance and belief. You think, you create, you implement and you move on. Let your ADHD empower you by seeing your unique self as a gift to be nurtured, not filed.

How does having ADHD affect you?
What are the positive aspects of your unique way of thinking?

inspiration + action
= creativity

MOTIVATED

Definition

A feeling of great interest in or enthusiasm for something, such as a goal, a cause or an injustice.

Signs & symptoms

Feeling fired up, driven, inspired and passionate.

Motivation and inspiration generate positive energy to encourage creativity and production. Successful people are motivated people. They don't just have an idea – they work at it and don't give up until they're satisfied. Motivated people aren't put off when things go wrong. They'll see it as a learning opportunity, a chance to refine and rethink. Other people's opinions won't put them off course. They stand apart from judgement, being more focused on their own actions and results. Motivation may start with a seed of an idea, and develop into a fantastic dream. Holding a vision before you is a powerful way to set a process in place. You can't know the route until you can see the destination. However, the vision alone isn't enough; it won't become real without a lot of effort and discipline.

Support & guidance Are you a motivated person, or do you tend to be demotivated by others? What kind of things inspire you? How do you make your own dreams come true? If you find it hard to be motivated, or find yourself in a situation that holds you back, make positive changes. Surround yourself with the right people and the right environment to support you. Perhaps you've tried hard in the past and things haven't worked out. What can you learn from those experiences? Are you willing to put in the work necessary to reach your goals, or do you expect too much from others? Ultimately, *you* are responsible for your successes and achievements. Let nothing get in the way of what you want, because everything is possible. Most importantly, give yourself positive thoughts to help you.

What holds you back from being more motivated?
What positive message can you give yourself?

I protect myself.

DEFENSIVE

Definition

Protecting yourself, physically or emotionally.

Signs & symptoms

Guarded; wary body language such as holding your arms around yourself; withdrawn, anxious; challenging to others.

People naturally defend themselves from perceived attacks, hurts and put-downs by using a variety of responses that can be seen as reasonable and rational or completely irrational, hurtful and confusing. We all want to stand up for ourselves and be assertive, true to our values and not be seen as weak. Using coping strategies to defend from anxiety or harm is quite understandable. However, people with fragile egos, a damaged sense of self or low self-esteem are often unable to *own* their own behaviours, accept themselves or take responsibility for their actions. This is where unconscious defence mechanisms come into play, such as projection, denial, blame, regression, passive aggression, withdrawal or fantasy.

Support & guidance Do you recognize yourself as defensive? Or are you in a relationship with someone so defensive that honest communication is difficult for fear of conflict? Either way, the important thing is not to be afraid to communicate how you feel or to show your vulnerability. A relationship that's worth having will be able to withstand disagreements and be accepting of mistakes. True love is unconditional and forgiving. It is healthier to have a disagreement than to withdraw emotionally. Defensive behaviour is childlike and doesn't address the real issues. If you find yourself sulking, manipulating or blaming others, take a long look in the mirror and be honest with yourself in a loving way. Otherwise, you end up hurting not just yourself but also those important to you. Being self-aware is key to your own happiness and life journey as a perfectly imperfect human being.

Are you a defensive person? How does it affect you?
What needs to change?

ATTACHMENT

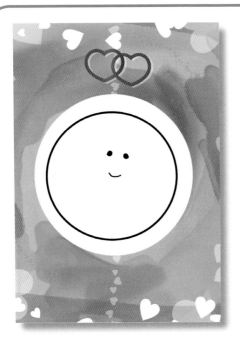

Definition

Being attached to someone or something.

Signs & symptoms

Feeling bound, devoted, close and loyal to someone; having strong feelings of connection towards material things, such as your home or possessions.

Attachment is a deep and long-term emotional bond that connects one person to another across time and space. Where the feeling is mutual, lasting commitment and friendships are formed, involving love, trust, fondness, compassion, empathy and respect. Where the feelings are not reciprocated, this can feel very painful and confusing. Attachment doesn't have to be reciprocal. One person may have an attachment to another which is not shared. Attachment Disorder is defined as a condition in which individuals have difficulty forming lasting relationships. They often show a lack of ability to be genuinely affectionate with others – and, typically, fail to develop a conscience. This stems from childhood abandonment or other childhood trauma which affects ability to trust others.

Support & guidance If you have attachment issues, then you might experience intense love while at the same time feeling insecure, judged, jealous and fearful of abandonment. Your relationships might swing from passionate connection to physical and/or emotional abuse. You will be aware that you push people away and then want them back again. You probably come across as needy and desperate. Are you afraid to be on your own? What stops you making healthy commitments to others? Your past doesn't need to determine your future. Be careful not to compare the people in your life now to those in your past. Everyone deserves a chance to be happy, including you. Let go of the need to be attached, then feel the difference.

Do you tend to have healthy or unhealthy attachments to others?
How can you let go of unhealthy attachments and become more independent?

What's going on?

JEALOUS

Definition

Being suspicious of a partner who you believe is more attracted to, or involved with, someone else; feeling resentful towards others who appear to have what you want.

Signs & symptoms

Relationship anxiety leading to internal or external conflict; controlling behaviour; possessiveness; comparing yourself to others, being confrontational, making assumptions, making demands, coming across as too needy.

Jealousy usually occurs in close relationships and friendships where there is an underlying fear of loss. This might involve your partner or best friend spending time with others, to the extent that you feel excluded. The actions may be quite innocent, but a jealous person will see the worst, imagine all sorts of conversations and scenarios, will mistrust the other party, and may challenge to the point of conflict, or keep quiet and remain unhappy and suspicious. Jealousy is exacerbated when honest communication is lacking, or mixed messages are given. Underlying issues include insecurity, lack of confidence and trust, feeling you're not good enough, previous rejection, unresolved anger or a history of failed relationships.

Support & guidance If you feel jealous, be careful not to let your actions be fuelled by irrational thinking. When you try too hard to find love or affection, this can be difficult for others to tolerate; it puts a lot of pressure on them and can push them away. This behaviour is unhealthy and dysfunctional and can become a self-fulfilling prophecy. You may find yourself having unhelpful thoughts about others being more attractive, successful, sexy, funny or better company than you. Jealousy can indicate where we're unhappy in our lives and teach us to take care of our own needs. Perhaps you're too dependent on others and are seeking constant approval or validation. Try to be more independent and see yourself as a 'whole', rather than someone else's other half.

What kind of jealous thoughts do you have?
How does jealousy affect your relationships?

REJECTED

Definition

Being dismissed, abandoned, ignored, passed over.

Signs & symptoms

Feeling disheartened and confused, not trusting others, fearing abandonment; can include feelings of anger, aggression and depression.

Feeling rejected can raise difficult emotions and lead to trust issues, health problems, lack of confidence and low self-esteem. Rejection might be a familiar feeling, especially if you first experienced it during childhood. When parents separate, it's important for children to know they're loved and wanted by both parents. Without this, they can feel that they're being abandoned or rejected. What's needed is a solid foundation that helps to build self-worth, identity and confidence. If security was lacking in your early years, you may have trust issues or feel insecure in relationships. This may lead to you ignoring warning signs, holding on to others or always trying to please. Perhaps you have a tendency to reject partners before they reject you. Rejection is hard to handle, especially if it comes out of the blue.

Support & guidance If you feel rejected by someone you love or care about, it doesn't mean there is anything wrong with you or that you've done something wrong. While it's useful to look at your own behaviour, try not to blame yourself or your actions. People come into and out of our lives for different reasons. If you have a strong sense that your relationship isn't working, communicate your doubts, your thoughts and your feelings to gain clarity. If you're meant to be together, then you will be. Losing someone you love is hard and it takes time to recover. In the meantime, be kind to yourself, accept yourself and be a loving soul to attract other loving souls into your life. Learn from the past so you can move forward with confidence and, most importantly, never reject yourself.

Have you ever decided not to continue a relationship or friendship? Why? How do you cope with feelings of rejection?

I SAY WHAT I MEAN

ASSERTIVE

Definition

A communication skill useful in relationships and in social and work situations; standing up for your own or others' needs or rights in a calm and positive way.

Signs & symptoms

Communicating thoughts, opinions and needs in a confident, assured way without being aggressive; speaking your mind without feeling guilty; knowing you have the right to your thoughts, feelings and opinions, as do others.

Assertive people can appear overly confident or forceful, but in fact what they are doing is being clear about their thoughts, opinions, feelings and boundaries. Some people go through life trying to please others, doing things for others and putting them first, perhaps through fear of rejection, or conflict. When you do this you are compromising yourself and your own happiness. It is perfectly OK to think about yourself and do what's right for you; otherwise, you can end up feeling resentful, guilty, overwhelmed, worried and anxious. It's also OK to say no if you don't want to do something, or you don't have time for it. People who are assertive gain more respect, because they are giving others a strong message.

Support & guidance If you feel you are not listened to or valued, and are taken advantage of, then only *you* can do something about it. Speaking up for yourself is important. Use strong, clear and consistent language. Keep your communication short and precise. Repeat your message. Don't feel the need to justify, defend or bend. Know your boundaries. We all have the right to put our priorities first, without needing to please others, and to express ourselves without one person needing to be right and the other wrong. Assertive communication values you and others, and helps clarify situations. Your needs are important; only you know what these truly are — so if you don't state them, how can others meet them? Never be afraid to speak your mind, because you deserve to be heard.

Do you believe you have the right to express your thoughts, feelings and opinions? What is it that you want to say?

Strong in Words.
Strong in Action.

STRONG

Definition

Strong-minded, confident, resistant, determined, focused; physically fit.

Signs & symptoms

Being calm and reliable when things go wrong; having an air of confidence; not getting flustered by emotions.

Strong people don't rely on the thoughts and opinions of others in order to make decisions. They have confidence in their own abilities and make the best of difficult situations. Rather than dwelling on mistakes, they learn from them. Self-accepting and tolerant of difference, they're not threatened by others; nor do they compare themselves in order to bolster or batter their own identity. People who have a strong mental attitude are determined and focused when it comes to making plans and getting things done, but can also go with the flow when a situation changes unexpectedly. They are quick to forgive, not bothering to hold onto resentments. They don't control but they are no pushover; they're not people-pleasers either, and have no problem cutting out negative people or bad situations. They don't worry about rejection, standing their ground alone, or with others.

Support & guidance Mental strength is positive thinking, seeing the best, looking beyond problems and allowing yourself to be vulnerable at times. When you're strong inside, nothing and no one can hurt you. If you would like to feel stronger, try regular exercise to increase your mental focus. When you feel physically fit, you'll be better able to face challenges. Adversity teaches us how to keep going when things get tough. First and foremost, you must love and accept yourself before you can be strong for others. Be clear about who you are, your values and your morals, and feel proud of yourself and your individuality. Be strong, self-controlled, firm and courageous. Unleash the wise lion.

In what ways are you strong?
How can you increase your strength?

CONFUSED

Definition

Disorientated, unbalanced, bewildered, unable to think clearly, having muddled thoughts.

Signs & symptoms

Dropping things, losing things, making mistakes, unable to make decisions or acting out of the norm.

Confusion occurs when mind and body are out of balance. It can happen because of stress, illness or relationship issues. Perhaps an argument has upset you or a decision needs to be made. Alternatively, if you're unwell or in pain, this can cause blurred thinking. When we're given information that turns out to be wrong, misleading or incomplete, it's hard to make sense of things. If you're working towards a goal and the objectives are unclear or change halfway through, this is likely to lead to confusion and lack of trust. It can also happen in relationships, when you're given mixed messages – saying one thing but doing something else: 'I love you, but actually I'm seeing someone else so let's just be friends.' Confused messages can mess with your head, leaving you feeling completely bewildered.

Support & guidance If you're confused a lot of the time, maybe you're taking on too much work or responsibility. Perhaps you have thoughts banging in your head, keeping you awake at night. Can you take some time for yourself to relax and unwind? Can you speak to someone about what is bothering you? Talking things through helps to make sense of things. If a relationship has caused you to feel unsure, try to communicate your thoughts and feelings in an honest way. Take responsibility for your actions while at the same time letting others know what it is that you need. You are important! Maybe it's you who isn't being clear and is creating further confusion down the line. If a message is unclear, check it out. Write things down to help you clarify. Look at all perspectives.

What causes you to feel confused? How can you clarify the situation?
What can you do to feel better?

SCATTY

Definition

Absent-minded and disorganized.

Signs & symptoms

Often being late; losing things; messy, being 'all over the place'; indecisive, unaware, clumsy and unfocused.

A scatty person might make arrangements to meet someone and not turn up, or turn up at the wrong time or in the wrong place. They'll ring friends and leave messages for them to call back, but never be available to take the call. They send a text to say, 'See you later', but nobody knows where. They book tables in restaurants but forget where they've booked. Scatty people might be highly attractive types who are very successful at getting jobs, winning contracts and making deals; however, they rarely carry through and usually need a team of people to do the work – a team who won't be given training or proper instructions, just a lot of mixed messages. Tasks will be last-minute and urgent, with everyone running round like crazy to reach a deadline that nobody is clear about. Invariably, the members of the team will get fed up and leave for more secure employment.

Support & guidance If you're scatty, you'll already know that people either get fed up with you and stop seeing you, or laugh at you in a loving way and see you as the airhead type who's definitely not to be relied upon. You can laugh at yourself and play up to this. You may think you'll learn how to be more organized, but it's very hard to do so, as your mind and personality just don't conform to what's expected. You know you do well in life, so changing won't be a priority. You're probably a very creative type, with lots of ideas that are totally 'outside the box' and may seem crazy to others. Never lose that creative side of yourself, because the scatty people of this world make life more interesting and fun.

What do you love most about your personality? What do you dislike about it? How could you be more organized?

GUILT

My conscience is getting to me

Definition

The feeling of a perceived wrongdoing, misconduct, sin or offence playing on your conscience.

Signs & symptoms

Shame, self-blame, remorse, sense of responsibility, rumination and preoccupation with thoughts; a weight on your shoulders.

We feel guilty when we know in our hearts and minds that we have done, or are doing, something fundamentally wrong that could hurt others. This could be intentional or unintentional. If intentional, and we have a sense of shame, guilt will follow. It shows we have a moral conscience, which is a guide to our own behaviour. For example, if you cheat on your partner, you may be able to justify it to yourself, but deep down you'll know that it's wrong. Your conscience is telling you! Violating your own values leads to feelings of remorse and regret, because you're guilty in your own eyes. In family relationships, we sometimes feel unhealthy irrational guilt for not giving enough or doing enough for others.

Support & guidance Guilt is a healthy warning sign that tells you something important about your behaviour and helps you take responsibility for your actions. It can be unhealthy when it involves you trying too hard to please others, and can be hard to manage if connected to an incident where you had little control. If you feel you've violated your moral standards, take responsibility for your actions, learn from it and move forward. Think about damage limitation! Communicate your regrets to others and apologize where needed. The ability to take ownership and say sorry for wrongdoings shows strength and a capacity to be empathic and mature. Don't dwell on the past – you don't live there now. Try not to beat yourself up; we all make mistakes. Be happy that you have a conscience that builds you up to the best you can be. A guilty conscience is the mother of self-awareness.

Who or what triggers your guilty feelings?
What can you do to clear your conscience?

Not letting go.

RESENTMENT

Definition

Bitter indignation at having been treated unfairly.

Signs & symptoms

Holding onto the past; angry, disappointed, dissatisfied, disheartened, disgusted; holding a grudge; feeling hateful.

When we feel resentment, we're holding onto negative emotional blocks, which is counter-productive to leading a happy, calm life. It's draining and stops you moving forward. People hold resentments for all sorts of reasons, towards people, organizations, or society as a whole for perceived wrongs or injustices. When people let us down, it's understandable to feel disappointed, hurt, angry and upset; but if a resolution isn't found straight away, by honest communication, the issue is held onto and internalized. It can become self-destructive, hurting you rather than the person you're angry with. We're all different; this doesn't make one person right and another wrong. Resentment is disempowering.

Support & guidance When things go wrong, we may take it personally, feel devalued and unloved or be negative about the situation. Imagine you're holding all your resentments in a bag. How heavy is it, and how much does it weigh you down? In order to lighten your load, you could think about letting go of the anger you feel towards others. Have you communicated your thoughts and feelings to those involved? Did you give them a chance to respond? Try looking at it from their perspective. Seeing the action as belonging to them, and not you, begs the question 'Do I need to feel bad because of someone else?' Resentment gives the power to them and doesn't change what happened. Life becomes easier when you learn to accept the apology you never got. How people treat you is down to them. How you respond is up to you! Don't let others' actions destroy your dreams.

What do you feel resentful about?
How does your resentment affect you?

JUDGED

Definition

Forming an opinion or conclusion about something or someone, or the feeling of being judged by another.

Signs & symptoms

Feeling criticized or questioned by another person; feeling that your character is under scrutiny.

When you feel judged, it's hard to be yourself and do what feels right for you, for fear that someone, somewhere, is going to make a judgement about you. This might be an individual who you've always felt judged by, such as a parent or sibling, or it might be a more general feeling of being judged by someone else connected to you in some way. When people talk about feeling judged, they're thinking about negative aspects of their behaviour, character or personality. Some people are their own harshest critics: 'I'm boring, selfish, stupid, always make mistakes, an addict, hopeless, helpless …' Self-deprecation is judging yourself, looking down on – and not approving of – yourself, and not feeling good enough.

Support & guidance Often, when we feel judged it is us making assumptions and doing the judging. We're not being a friend to ourselves, talking to ourselves negatively, which can start a cycle of judgements that leads to low self-esteem and lack of confidence. Perhaps you're judgemental of others. What is it that you don't like about them? Are you guilty of the same thing? Let go of judging others. Look at them kindly, in the way you'd like others to see you. We all need to be free to do our thing, to grow, make mistakes, learn, fall, get up again, get stronger. If you're criticized by others, thank them for their opinion and reflect. You don't need to justify yourself. It doesn't make them right or you wrong. Concentrate, instead, on being yourself, having fun, focusing on your strengths, talents and potential. More kindness and less judgement from now on!

Who judges you the most?
What are the judgements on you and how true are they?

ANNOYED

Definition

Slightly angry, irritated, bothered, uptight, frustrated.

Signs & symptoms

Being bad-tempered, impatient, aggravated by small things, taking it out on others or using negative body language.

People who get annoyed easily tend to be those with high expectations, little patience, fixed ideas and who like to be in control. When life doesn't flow as you'd like, this can set off a chain of negative thoughts, moans, exasperations, huffs and puffs. It's the little things that annoy: when you tell somebody to do something again and again and they *still* get it wrong; when you're waiting patiently in a queue and someone comes along and puts themselves right at the front; when you arrive early at the station for a meeting to hear that your train is delayed. Grrr. Or perhaps you get annoyed with yourself, because you're not living the life you want or keeping on top of your workload. Or, you feel that you're not being listened to or that your needs aren't met.

Support & guidance If you're the kind of person who expects things to always go your way, then you probably spend a lot of time being disappointed. How do you cope when things are out of your control? It's easy to let things get to you, but you need to get over the idea that life 'should' run smoothly. The only thing we can control is, in fact, ourselves – not others, nor external events. Think how lovely life would be if you didn't get annoyed and became more accepting. If things get delayed, so be it. If you're in a traffic jam, turn on some music and sing. If you arrive late, you'll still get there – it's not the end of the world. Most importantly, don't be annoyed at yourself. Be realistic, be patient with others, because you don't know their story. Take your time, go slower and breathe deeply.

What kinds of thing annoy you?
Do you have very high expectations of others, or in life generally?

sick inside

DISGUST

Definition

A feeling of revulsion or strong disapproval aroused by something unpleasant or offensive.

Signs & symptoms

Being annoyed or dissatisfied with behaviour or situations where you expected more.

Disgust is a feeling that sickens you inside. It could be related to something visual, such as a filthy mess or food that has long gone off; all senses come into play – sight, hearing, taste, smell and touch. Where disgust relates to a situation, it can be harder to stomach, as you may feel powerless to do anything about it. The media is full of news that can horrify, appal and fill us with a sense of disbelief at the way humans can behave towards each other. Where violations take place against you, or those you love, there can be a real sense of injustice that can lead to you taking steps to put right the perceived wrongs. Disgust is one of those emotions that can result in positive action, whether to join a protest, political party or support group, or perhaps a discreet conversation in someone's ear is all that's needed.

Support & guidance If you can take action against something that disgusts you, then do so. If your feelings connect to a specific person, try to speak to them about the impact of their behaviour – make them aware, so they can choose to do something about it (or not). We're not always going to agree with, or approve of, the actions of others. Be careful not to judge before knowing the full story. People sometimes get things wrong through ignorance rather than malice. Give them the benefit of the doubt by honest communication. If your disgust is on a more global scale, make your voice heard for the greater good. We all need to stand up for what's right, and help create more peace, compassion and understanding in the world. Make your words count. Aim to be delighted, not disgusted.

What kinds of things disgust you?
What do you do about it?

I can't believe I did that.

SHAME

Definition

A feeling of humiliation or distress relating to an action that doesn't fit with moral code; feeling fundamentally flawed in some way.

Signs & symptoms

Feeling guilt or embarrassment about your actions and reactions and being very self-critical.

We feel shame when our actions don't fit the image we have of ourselves or that we want others to see. It ties in with guilt, but is different. Guilt relates to behaviour; shame is more a feeling about self. You can feel shame and still continue to behave in shameful ways, which is confusing – it can feel like you've pressed the self-destruct button. Over-eating, or addiction to drugs, alcohol or sex, causes shame and leads to self-criticism, self-loathing and vulnerability. People who feel shame tend to have low opinions of themselves, and every act that they regret is confirmation they're a bad person, or not good enough. Fear of judgement can lead to feelings of vulnerability and weakness. Then there is global shame – the feeling that, as a community or society, we could do more to help others.

Support & guidance Nobody is perfect, and failings help us learn about ourselves and what feels right or wrong. Understanding shame helps to build our moral guidelines. Experiencing shame shows that you have empathy, consideration and a conscience and that you can be self-reflective. At times, we all act, say or do things that go against the person we think we are, or would like to be seen as. Think about whether your feeling of shame comes from guilt about an action, or is more about the way you view yourself. You're likely to be your strongest critic, so cut yourself some slack. You're human like the rest of us, not perfect, just striving to do – and be – your best, so be compassionate towards your imperfections; we all have them. Be understanding and kind to yourself – you're worth it.

How does shame affect your life?
What can you do to feel pride instead?

ABANDONED

Definition

Being deserted or left by somebody close or a loved one.

Signs & symptoms

Feeling uncared for, rejected, let down, deeply hurt and disappointed.

Feelings of abandonment often stem from childhood experience. In the early years, healthy bonding and attachment is vital to development, and when this fails insecurity sets in. Very young children feel emotions but are unable to intellectualize or verbalize. We all need to feel secure and cared for, so we can grow into healthy, loving adults. Things go wrong for many reasons, such as relationship break-ups, mental health issues and addiction. When a child is abandoned, physically or emotionally, this leaves a mark, a damage, a wound deep within. If this abandonment is accompanied by other traumatic experiences, the effects can be long-lasting, and can manifest as trust issues, neediness, vulnerability, addiction, negative self-talk or low self-esteem.

Support & guidance Feeling abandoned can affect confidence, faith and trust in others and the world. When things go wrong in relationships, it can re-trigger early feelings of abandonment, loss and rejection – a pattern repeating itself. The more it happens, the more the abandoned person blames themselves, which affects the energy they put out into the world and future behaviours. Perhaps you are needy, controlling or high maintenance. What is it that you feel and what is it that you need? Try and communicate this to others, so they can reassure you. Break the cycle by learning to trust again. Listen to your intuition if it's telling you that things are not right, but don't forget to check out the evidence before you make assumptions about others, or abandon them before they leave you.

Do you believe you are worth loving?
What needs to happen for you to trust again?

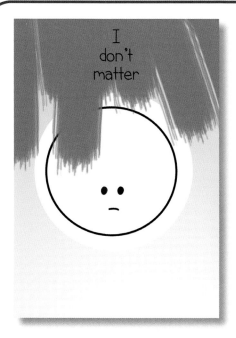

WORTHLESS

Definition

Having no value, use or good qualities.

Signs & symptoms

Feeling inadequate and inferior, with negative self-beliefs and thinking. Low self-esteem.

People who feel worthless have a strong sense that they are unimportant to others, they are not worth listening to, their opinions are not valid, their work not noticed and their efforts not appreciated. Feelings of worthlessness develop over a period of time. It's very upsetting to feel like you don't matter, and this can cause anxiety, stress and depression. Some typical thoughts might be: 'I'm not that good at this or that'; 'I'm a boring person, so I'm not worth listening to'; 'I'm not that good at my job — I'm just scraping by hoping no one will notice me'; 'I wish I was a better parent/wife/husband'; 'Others are brighter, smarter and more outgoing than me — in fact, I'm really not that great.'

Support & guidance When you feel worthless, you are in fact giving yourself strong statements that say 'I am not worthy' and 'I don't matter'. You are probably also a negative thinker, in a loop and spiral of negativity. Try to be more of a friend to yourself, and start changing your thoughts to more positive, helpful statements about who you are, your strengths, your skills, your achievements, your qualities and talents, and all of the ways you deserve to lead a good, fulfilled life. Thinking about what you can offer to others and how you can be of service is a great way to feel good about yourself, too. Don't reject praise; instead, be grateful and humble. We are all valuable and unique members of the human race. Your journey is ahead of you, so make it worthwhile.

What negative thoughts do you have about yourself?
What would your best friend say about you?

DESIRE DESIRE DESIRE

ENVY

Definition

Feeling or showing resentment towards someone because of their achievements, possessions, luck or perceived advantages; coveting what others have.

Signs & symptoms

Jealousy, bitterness, spite, having bad feelings towards someone who is doing well, rather than being pleased for them. Envious people sometimes find it hard to be self-reflective or objective about situations.

Envy is one of the most difficult and destructive of emotions. It comes from a sense of insecurity, unworthiness and low self-esteem. It is wanting what others have – money, luck, love, or better relationships, job prospects, cultural ties … You may think, 'Why them? They don't deserve it – I do.' It can be overwhelming, frustrating and painful to watch 'your life' being played out by others and can lead to you blaming others for your fortune, rather than taking responsibility for it. When our envy is fuelled, it can result in us spoiling things for others, tainting reputations, embellishing facts, inflicting misfortune, making false claims, gossiping, openly criticizing or lying for our own advantage. At the very worst, an envious person will try to outdo the target of their envy by taking undue credit, bullying, harassing, manipulating or ganging up on them, or by discriminating against them in some way.

Support & guidance Are you sometimes overwhelmed by envy? What is it others have that you want? Some things can't be changed, but others can. Perhaps it is *you* who is holding you back more than anything or anyone else. If you find yourself wanting what others have and hating them for it, take a few breaths. Now look in the mirror and see your own worth, count your talents and blessings, and make a plan of how to achieve your own goals and aspirations … because you can do it! Believe in and appreciate yourself and look kindly at others who walk their path – which may not have been an easy one. Success comes to those who work hard and focus their energy in a positive direction. Can you do that?

How has envy affected your life?
Do you have envious thoughts? What are they?

I have so much to be thankful for.

GRATITUDE

Definition

Appreciation, connection and acknowledgement of all the beautiful blessings that surround you.

Signs & symptoms

Conscious awareness of the big and the small things that bring joy and happiness into your life, and being thankful for them.

Gratitude is the act of noticing and acknowledging all that you feel blessed with. For many people, the default mode is to moan and complain – about the weather, work, and so on. Other more positive types count their blessings, appreciating the beauty of a blue sky, or flowers in springtime. They might start the day with a meditation or yoga, to encourage a positive energy flow and a strong, clear connection to the joys of life. Feeling grateful brings a sense of well-being and warmth. When we appreciate what we have, we feel satisfied externally, and internally our bodies will flow in natural rhythm. Gratitude subconsciously activates positive neurons within, for a healthy mind, body and soul. It helps us to radiate calmness and positivity, thereby welcoming more of those traits into our lives.

Support & guidance Don't let life get you down. Instead, let it lift you up. Each day is a gift that has been given to you. Make a pact with yourself to consciously connect with gratitude on a daily basis. Cultivate your response to each day as if it were the first and last day of your life. Appreciate the moment, open your eyes to everything that surrounds you. Try keeping a gratitude diary and list three things each day that you are blessed with – from family and friends to hearing birds sing or watching the sunrise. Be in the moment, mindful of what's happening around you, what you see, sense, feel, smell. Open your heart to drink the experience of life; let it flow through you. Soon you will realize that life is a blessing and you're part of a wonderful web of interconnectedness. Let gratitude be your attitude.

What are you grateful for?
How do you think counting your blessings will help you?

GRIEF

Definition

The psychological-emotional experience that follows the loss of a loved one. Symptoms can also accompany other types of loss, such as job, home, relationship, status or income.

Signs & symptoms

Intense sorrow involving emotional, mental and sometimes physical pain; anguish, distress, crying, disruption of normal behaviour and circadian rhythms, shock, disbelief, difficulty accepting, guilt, remorse, regret, social withdrawal.

Grief is an intensely painful destabilizing experience following the loss of a loved one. Patterns of grief go in stages (these stages are variable) and can last for many years. Stage 1 (first 2 weeks): shock (sobbing, physical pain, shivering, restricted throat); numbness (feeling lost, isolated, detached, withdrawn and clinging); denial (disbelief, expecting the loved one to return, constant reminiscing, hallucinations). Stage 2 (1–3 months): yearning, searching, anxiety, anger, guilt and loneliness. Stage 3 (8–9 months): depression, apathy, loss of identity, mitigation, stigma (loss of friends/feeling ostracized). Stage 4 (1–2 years or longer): acceptance and healing. Relationship break-ups are also devastatingly painful: to know that the person you love with all your heart and soul is still out there, but unavailable to you. Your hearts no longer beat as one.

Support & guidance There is no right or wrong way to grieve. Take each day as it comes. Seek as much support as you can from friends and family. If you notice changes in your appetite, energy and sleep, try as hard as you can to keep to a healthy routine. The mourning period may feel dark and lonely, and there will be times when you can't see past surviving each day. Take care of yourself; try to continue with normal activities as much as possible, such as working or looking after family. Listen to music for comfort and memories, but also to lift your mood. Remember, true love never dies and people live on in beautiful memories that can be cherished for years to come.

What are your most treasured memories of your loved one? If you could have one more day with them, what would you do and what would you say?

Love is everything - the key to life, the colour of my heart

LOVE

Definition

*A strong connection towards someone
or something, at the deepest level
of the soul; being in love.*

Signs & symptoms

*Stars in your eyes, rose-coloured spectacles,
excitement, passion, affection, strong
physical attraction, bonding, obsession.
Feeling fulfilled with a partner or other
activity that brings great joy.*

Love is the answer to many of life's problems. When we're loved unconditionally as children, we grow up feeling secure and safe, with freedom to be creative and adventurous. Being loved teaches us to love and care for others in kind and compassionate ways. Love is commitment, purity, unselfishness, trust and honesty, helping one another, respecting difference, reaching out for your dreams, the connection of two hearts, a soulmate, family, sharing your deepest secrets. Magical, romantic and enchanting, it takes our breath away, obsesses our thoughts, electrifies our physical senses. Love isn't always easy and is some-times so painful that it breaks your heart. Unrequited love is the impossible dream of limerent togetherness. Is it better to have loved and lost than never to have loved at all?

Support & guidance How does love touch your life? Are you loving towards yourself? If you don't love yourself, you'll always be chasing after people who don't love you, either. Loving yourself will bring you the confidence to know that you're whole and perfect. You don't need another half. Choose to support yourself in kind ways. Find activities you love, eat food you love, give your love to others or to a pet that will love you back unconditionally. Honour yourself with positive thoughts. Embrace yourself with arms wide open, rejoice in your power and strength. Release all past disappointments and hurts. Forgive yourself when needed. Universal love is freely available, so open your channel to receive. Be the conduit for change, not just for yourself but for the wider world too. Let the love flow.

*How do you define love?
How can you live in a more loving way?*

ANGER

Definition

Feeling or showing strong annoyance, displeasure, rage or hostility.

Signs & symptoms

Acting in an aggressive way, shouting, yelling, banging around, or giving the silent treatment and seeking revenge, or focusing the anger inwards onto the self.

Anger as a primary emotion is a healthy response to situations that appear unwanted or unfair. It can be brought on by tiredness, hunger or stress. As a secondary emotion, we become angry when we're frustrated or feel criticized and under threat, such as when others treat us disrespectfully, don't meet our expectations, are selfish, ignorant or arrogant. Then there is the anger at the self, for not being good, clever or smart enough. Anger can lead to self-deprecation and a spiral of negative thinking, for saying the wrong thing or acting irrationally, or for not performing to the best of your ability, being lazy or disorganized.

Support & guidance If your anger gets you in trouble, try taking deep breaths or walk away to calm down. All feelings are temporary. Communicate your thoughts and feelings to those involved when the anger has subsided – listen to their side, too. If you don't express yourself, anger stays within and can fester into a big ball of resentment. If you often feel angry but it is non-specific, you may be in a loop of negative thinking. To break the pattern, make a list of all the things that bother you. What are your thoughts about these issues? How true are they? Look for evidence. Now see what other, more helpful, positive thoughts you can have. Holding onto anger is self-destructive, and you are the one to suffer. This gives away a lot of your power. Rein it in, take control, learn to accept the past. You don't need to forget, but forgiveness sets you free. Try the art of non-reaction – observe others, but don't be a participant in the drama or suffer for their actions.

What kinds of things make you angry?
How do you manage your anger?

We all make mistakes.

FORGIVING

Definition

To release feelings of anger or resentment towards another.

Signs & symptoms

No longer being affected by others; being more tolerant, understanding and accepting of the past.

There are times when we feel let down, disrespected, ignored, bullied, slighted or outraged by another's behaviour. Someone may have hurt or offended us in some way, either intentionally or inadvertently. We usually feel this most when it involves a close family member, friend or partner. People do things for all kinds of reasons, and some things just don't make sense. Perhaps your partner has consistently behaved in an upsetting way towards you over a period of time, or committed the ultimate betrayal. We all make mistakes on our life journeys. We're all fallible and irrational at times. Forgiveness is the process of letting go of what has hurt you: to do so will bring a sense of lightness and relief.

Support & guidance Our expectations of others can never be fully met, because we all have different opinions about what is right or wrong. When people act against our morals, it can feel unfair, or even abusive. Forgiveness comes from accepting difference and an ability to release resentment for what has happened. It doesn't condone behaviour or make it acceptable, nor does it mean you need to forget. What happens to us helps us to learn for the future, to make choices and decisions, which might include walking away from negative people, working on your own boundaries and being more assertive. Holding onto anger and resentment is self-destructive – it doesn't hurt or harm others, but only causes internal pain that can eat away at you. Forgiveness of others brings freedom and puts an end to internal suffering. Forgiveness is the key to inner peace.

Do you find it easy or difficult to forgive people?
What do you see as the benefit of forgiveness?

DEPRESSED

Definition

An illness of mind and body with fluctuating moods and emotions; feeling despondent and unhappy, which can prevent sufferers from leading a normal life.

Signs & symptoms

Lack of interest or pleasure in daily activities, significant weight loss or gain, insomnia or excessive sleeping, lack of energy, inability to concentrate, feelings of worthlessness or excessive guilt, suicidal, anxious.

Depression can feel like someone's pulled a switch. You're in the dark and it's hard to see a way out. You exist but you don't exist; you may have an intense feeling of nothingness where you want to hide under the duvet, not talk to others, withdraw from life. It often follows stressful events such as bereavement, a break-up or redundancy. Advice and help from others may feel supportive but can be hard to act on. You remember a time when life was different, when you ate properly, exercised, had fun. Your low energy and negative mindset may be hard to understand and confusing, because this isn't 'you'. There are different stages of depression, from feeling down to a full-on severe illness where it's hard to function normally. Moods can vary, and concentration and decisions become harder.

Support & guidance Many people suffer from depression at some point in life and recover when the time is right. It's not a sign of weakness, although it can leave you weak. It can be hard for others to understand because it's not visible. Depression is a sign that you need 'deep rest', so listen to your body. In time it will lift, like a cloud, and once it's gone, it's gone. Rather than trying to fight your depression, acknowledge it and think about the small steps you can take to beat it. But don't push too hard; recovery can be a slow process. Visit your doctor for support and talk to a counsellor to release your feelings and find strategies. Regular exercise will increase your endorphins and wholesome food will fill your empty tank. Don't be afraid to ask for help; there are people who love and care about you.

How has depression affected your life?
What has helped you in the past? What will help you now?

I am curious about life and all of its possibilities!

INTERESTED

Definition

Showing curiosity or concern about something or someone; loving to learn and find out more about others and the world.

Signs & symptoms

Being inquisitive, asking questions, reading a lot, showing enthusiasm for ideas.

Life is full of interesting things and each day presents new opportunities for learning. The media brings daily stories about what's going on in the world, but how much of that do we take a real interest in? Being interested is wanting to find out more, being curious about a subject or person that invites more attention. It could be something connected with your life at present, such as a hobby you want to pursue or an illness you need to know more about. It might be that you're thinking about a career change and want information about the options available. You might show interest in a person because you want to get to know them better, are hoping for a friendship, a connection, a network, support, some information or even a role model.

Support & guidance How interesting are you? Perhaps you'd like to be *more* interesting, and therefore need to expand your horizons. Being open to new possibilities is a great way to inspire curiosity and learning. When you show interest in other people, they are more likely to show interest in you. This will help to build strong connections. What are you interested in, and do you pursue those interests? If you were on a desert island, who would you choose to be there with you and why? We are all interesting in some way, even though we may *feel* boring. Think of three interesting things about you and your life. How would you describe yourself? The world is a place of endless curiosity and interest: be open to life and all its possibilities to enrich your own life journey.

What kind of things do you find interesting?
Do you take advantage of the opportunities that life presents to you?

HATE

Definition

A feeling of intense dislike towards someone or something.

Signs & symptoms

Revolted, disgusted, angry, displeased, hesitant, hostile.

Hate can be triggered internally (not getting your own way) or externally (the behaviour of others). It can grow from anger and hurt or painful acts by others, whether emotional, physical or sexual. Or perhaps you hate someone who has bullied you over a period of time. This kind of hatred leads to resentment, demotivation and thoughts of revenge; it has energy and strength, but never brings happiness. Then there is the blind hatred connected to difference, racism, religion, sexual orientation, extremism, misogyny; small-minded, insidious and dangerous, it can influence others and preys on vulnerable minds. There is a thin line between love and hate, and in relationships hate is part of the separation process.

Support & guidance When hatred is held deep within, it's toxic and damaging to the soul. It's a form of self-harm and actually gives power to the target of your hate. Do you see them as being more important than you? Does their behaviour count more than your reaction? If you have ever felt hated yourself, what did you do to deserve it? It's human nature to seek love, nurturing and respect; to feel valued and appreciated for who you are. It's not what happens to us in life that creates problems, but our beliefs surrounding those experiences. Check your negative thinking. Look for evidence to prove or disprove your theories. Become an observer rather than a participant. Most importantly, free yourself from your hateful thoughts and allow that energy to dissipate, making room for love, compassion and understanding. When you hate someone, they don't feel your pain – *you* do!

Does hatred have a space in your life? How does it affect you?
What needs to happen for you to let go?

I smile. I laugh. I bounce.

HAPPY

Definition

Content, cheerful, joyful, carefree, untroubled, delighted; feeling fulfilled internally, from appreciating the smallest gifts in life as well as the large successes.

Signs & symptoms

Beaming, glowing, eyes shining, bouncing with energy.

Happiness means different things to different people. It's not something you go out and get; it comes from within. Being happy is a natural state, not necessarily a response or reaction to other events. It doesn't need to come because of something else; happiness isn't a destination – it's the way you experience the journey along the way. Modern life, fuelled by consumerism, gives us false realities about what will make us happy. The truth is that you can't buy happiness in a store or online. When you feel happy, you are more likely to be content, satisfied, confident, and be more willing to help, advise and support others.

Support & guidance Your outlook on life is vital to how you feel, and building a more upbeat, positive attitude is a first step towards feeling happier. It can be as simple as waking up slowly and enjoying the moment, taking time to eat breakfast and savouring every mouthful, smiling inwardly to yourself and outwardly to others. Be grateful for your life; for the small and the bigger things. Recognize what you already have, rather than focusing on what is lacking. Notice the beauty of nature, the tastes and aromas of cooking, the sounds of children playing. Rewire your mind towards more positive thoughts for positive outcomes. Delete all negative thinking – all it does is hold you back. Meditate on a daily basis, focus on your breath for 10 minutes a day. Find light and joyous moments in dark situations. Let go of judgements and expectations of others. Don't waste time worrying about the future or the past; be in the *now* and breathe happy thoughts.

What brings you happiness?
What advice would you give to others on being happy?

REGRET

if only

Definition

A feeling of sadness, shame or disappointment over something that you've done or failed to do.

Signs & symptoms

Feeling guilty and bad about yourself, wishing things had happened differently.

Life can be full of regrets – the paths you could have taken, the career you could have had, the holidays you've missed out on and all of the opportunities that have passed you by. Regret is feeling bad about an action that you have taken or could have taken. In relationships, it might be about things you've said that caused pain, or perhaps you've stayed too long for fear of change – and are now regretting it. You may have lost good friendships because of your forgetfulness, thoughtlessness, bad moods, unwise actions or even betrayal of trust. Or, perhaps you've been let down by someone and you truly regret that you're no longer close. People often talk about having wasted years in a job that is unfulfilling, where they feel undervalued and undermined.

Support & guidance Do you want your life to be full of regrets, or full of pride and happy memories? When you're old and look back to the past, what regrets do you think you might have? Make a list. Now think about the positive actions you can take to achieve a life to be proud of. This might be about taking drastic steps that take you out of your comfort zone, or it might be simpler steps like pursuing more hobbies or having a better work/life balance. Perhaps you need to have difficult conversations with certain people, to put right some wrongs. Inaction often comes from lack of confidence in our own ability to communicate effectively or to be honest about our feelings. Have faith in yourself and others that things can be better.

What regrets do you have?
How can you make sure your life is no longer full of regrets?

I take life as it comes.

There are some things you just can't change.

ACCEPTANCE

Definition

Being OK with the reality of a situation. Acknowledgement of self and others.

Signs & symptoms

Understanding that things are the way they are, coming to terms with it and moving on; accepting life as it is and feeling peace within.

When we feel stressed and anxious, it's usually because of a resistance in the mind and body between the way things are and the way we want them to be. In a relationship, you may want your partner to behave in a certain way, and spend time and energy trying to change them. This is wasted energy – there's little you can do to control others. In the same way, if you're unhappy at work, you may need to accept that the job is *not* for you. There may be times when you're trying hard to push things in your direction, but you just end up stressed and burnt out. When things happen that are beyond our control, like a bereavement or natural disaster, there is a grief process to go through before we can accept the situation. This takes time, but eventually life will move on and the pain will heal.

Support & guidance Acceptance of yourself, your abilities, your appearance and your personality will help you to know that you deserve to be treated well, to be listened to and to have opportunities to shine. We can't change who we are, but we *can* change the way we view ourselves. We can't change others, but we *can* decide who is part of our life. We can't control outside events, but we *can* control whether we accept them calmly or not. Acceptance of people as they are, situations that arise and life in general allows you to be free from resistance: you can see the world objectively, and you can make good choices for yourself. That is empowering and, through this calm strength, life will take on new meaning and your creativity and abundance will flow.

Do you find it hard or easy to accept when life doesn't go your way? How can you be more accepting?

I expected more.

DISAPPOINTED

Definition

Unhappiness caused by someone or something failing to meet your hopes or expectations.

Signs & symptoms

Feeling disheartened, down-hearted and let down.

Disappointment can come from unmet expectations in all areas of life, including with yourself. We disappoint ourselves when we don't stick to our goals or behave in line with our morals. We might constantly berate ourselves for not doing this or that. Generally, we fail to live up to our own expectations when they are too high or are unrealistic. It's hard not to feel disappointment when you're let down by others, especially those you love and trust. If you find yourself consistently disappointed with certain people in your life, perhaps it's time to reassess those relationships. In a work setting, disappointment can lead to demotivation, low energy and stress. If you're not feeling valued, listened to, supported and encouraged to reach your potential, you're in the wrong environment for your well-being.

Support & guidance Being disappointed shows that you care, and that you believed in a situation or person. Perhaps things didn't turn out the way you wanted, or that person let you down. The best way to avoid disappointment is to let go of expectations or high, unrealistic demands on yourself or others. Seek out those that support your ideals of partnership and friendship and cut the ties with people that bring negativity into your life. Honest communication with others will lead to less disappointment and deeper connection. Rise above judgements, respect yourself and be the person you wish to see reflected back at you. You won't see your next chapter if you keep ruminating on the past. Move on in loving self-compassion and kindness.

What disappoints you?
What do you need to do to change things?

Bring it on ...

HOPEFUL

Definition

Feeling optimistic about a future event or outcome.

Signs & symptoms

Confident, positive, free from worry, looking on the bright side.

Hope is that eternal optimism that keeps you moving in a positive direction, even in the face of adversity. It's the light that shines in the darkness, it's confidence in yourself and trust in the universe. People that are hopeful believe in good endings. In the face of illness, having hope makes a powerful difference to your state of mind and the way you view your recovery. Hope doesn't entertain bad news; it focuses on being well again. Hope carries a very powerful energy into your whole body to promote healing and well-being. In the face of redundancy, a hopeful person will look at opportunities for a life change, and will be forward-thinking rather than dwelling in a state of resentment. A hopeful person tends to be more accepting of life.

Support & guidance To be more hopeful, retrain your mindset by starting each day with positive affirmations … Things will go well; I look forward to what the future holds; I can do it; I think *big*; I keep going until I succeed; I am well; I have courage and strength; I believe in myself and trust in my abilities to succeed; I know what is right for me; I can only work on myself – let others do their thing; I can do whatever I put my mind to; I can learn; I can accept responsibility; I welcome change; My determination is strong and powerful; I am a magnet for positivity; I am grateful for all blessings; I am passionate about X, Y or Z; What will be will be; Tomorrow is another day; I breathe calm and feel relaxed; I am capable; I deserve to be happy. Guide yourself to happiness, contentment and dream fulfilment.

Do you focus on what can go wrong, or what will go right?
What are your hopes for your own future?

Where is it? I need it NOW!

ADDICTED

Definition

Physical and/or mental dependence on a substance or behaviour that is self-harming and self-abusive.

Signs & symptoms

Obsessional, infatuated, fixated, hooked; loss of control; anxiety, depression, agitation, fatigue, loss of appetite.

Addiction is complicated; whether it's to drugs, alcohol, food or sex, it can be very difficult to live with, not just for yourself but for those who love you. The cycle of addiction runs something like this: feeling normal and calm; internal frustration and agitation; obsessing; loss of control; using/abusing to relieve cravings or fill the gaps inside yourself; feeling momentary satisfaction followed by shame, guilt, fear and regret, which can then feed into negative thoughts about yourself, your value and self-esteem. You may make promises to yourself, and others, to stop the behaviour, but despair and despondency may soon set in when triggers and challenges arise. The story of every addict will be different, and it's important to respect the individual. Most addicts wish to just feel 'normal'. Many talk of feeling empty within, having a void in the soul.

Support & guidance In order to face recovery, the time has to be right for you, which may mean hitting rock bottom. Everyone has a choice, but if your addiction is out of control, then join a fellowship programme or seek professional help. Recovery is a real possibility, but if you continue on the same path, the direction is clear: more of what you already have. Think about how your life could be without acting on your addiction. If you didn't listen to that voice within, what could you do instead? To heal yourself, get tough – you *can* do it. Take a day at a time. If you're in a relationship with an addict, put strong boundaries in place so their dysfunction doesn't become yours. Tough love is a powerful place to start.

How would your life be without addiction?
What needs to happen for you to make the necessary changes?

I don't even want to talk about it.

DREAD

Definition

An anticipation, strong feeling or fear that something bad will — or might — happen.

Signs & symptoms

Feeling anxious or sick inside about a future scenario and outcome, or spending life in a state of non-enjoyment and without fulfilment.

Do you dread waking up each morning? Are you doing the same thing day in, day out and expecting a different result? Do you go on the same crowded train each day to a job you don't like, working with a boss who doesn't appreciate you or promotes over you without seeing your worth? Or are you in a relationship with a partner who abuses you, puts you down, doesn't listen to you, ignores or talks over you, is passive-aggressive, controlling, dominating or self-centred? Of course, if someone is very ill or has been involved in a tragic accident, incident or trauma, the feeling of dread is a perfectly reasonable and rational response. You pray with all your heart that the news will be good, that the outcome will be favourable, but deep in your heart and soul there is a readiness for the worst.

Support & guidance Dread is a human response that helps us prepare for perceived and expected realities. Whatever you're going through, focusing on positive outcomes and practical solutions can help. Can you control what can happen? If not, do what feels right. If your dread is more the everyday type, visualize the future you wish to see and think about what you need to do to make powerful changes, so you can live the life you feel you deserve. Rather than dreading, start creating, being inspired, nurturing yourself and feeling excited about possibilities. Value yourself for who you are, and remember that every day starts with a new opportunity. You are the director of your movie. Start saying yes, even if that takes you out of your comfort zone. Every yes offers a chance to discover something new.

What do you dread?
What, if anything, can you do about it?

TOXIC SHAME

Definition

An excessive, unhealthy level of shame that causes emotional and interpersonal dysfunction, insecurity and low self-esteem.

Signs & symptoms

An overall assessment of the self as being worthless, inadequate, bad and unlovable; manifests in anger, helplessness and guilt.

Toxic shame tends to occur in people who've grown up in chaotic, dysfunctional family systems, cultures of violence or homes where one or both parents has addiction or mental health issues. Where children are abused, emotionally or physically, this causes long-term damage to feelings of identity, made worse if they are told off, criticized or inappropriately blamed. There may be secrets within the family that can't be shared with others. These secrets become the 'shames' that are held within. This type of shame runs deep and can manifest as feeling defective, not good or smart enough, self-loathing and self-deprecation. It can also lead to self-harm, addiction, eating disorders, depression and mood disorders.

Support & guidance Breaking through toxic shame requires self-awareness and reflection of how your current thinking affects your life. Whatever happened to you in the past, the messages you received from others and the experiences that have formed you so far don't have to determine your future. Learned behaviour can be unlearned. Cultivate new positive thoughts and habits. Try to stay away from blame and resentment. Be there for yourself, for that little child inside you who needs to be loved, cared for, encouraged, supported and fully accepted. Seek support to talk through your thoughts and feelings, learn to trust yourself and your instincts so you can move forward, make mistakes along the way and encourage yourself on every step you take in your life journey. Take compliments with grace and treat yourself to nice things.

What do you feel proud of?
What positive affirmations can you give yourself?

thank you for everything

BLESSED

Definition

*An awareness of all the good in your life.
A joyful feeling of happiness.*

Signs & symptoms

*A feeling of sheer bliss, contentment
and inner peace; feeling at one with
the flow of life; gratitude for the
smallest things.*

Counting your blessings every day will keep you grounded and bring happiness into your life. We are all blessed in many ways – with family, friends, children, grandchildren, and life itself. Blessed to eat, to drink, to feel the security of the ground beneath our feet. Blessed to see this beautiful world, feel the sun on our faces, the cold of the snow in winter. Blessed to love and be loved. Blessed for the lessons we learn each day. Blessed with education, to be able to read and write. Blessed with humour and laughter. Blessed with music, dancing, creativity and expression. Our blessings are many and will multiply with positive intention for joy and happiness for ourselves and others.

Support & guidance When you count your blessings, you are focusing, in a conscious, positive way, on your life in the present moment; being grateful for all you are and all you can be. Can you count your blessings on one hand, two hands, or is a list needed? Rather than thinking about the things that are wrong in your life, or the things you don't have, how about connecting to what you have been blessed with? Many people put happiness on hold, while they wait for their situation to change, their work to improve or for people to change their behavior in some way. They live in a negative state of lack, rather than in a positive state of abundance. Abundance brings more abundance. Wealth brings more wealth. Health brings more health. Being a loving person will bring more love into your life. Connect to your blessings for a Blessed Life.

*What are your blessings?
How will counting your blessings improve your life?*

Frustration has turned me from a normally peaceful, loving person into an irrational, angry one.

FRUSTRATED

Definition

Annoyance, distress, feeling prevented from progressing, succeeding or being fulfilled; sexual tension.

Signs & symptoms

Feeling upset, angry, exasperated or impatient with others or a situation.

Feeling frustrated is so annoying. You've done what you can to move things forward but someone or something is stopping you. This can be demotivating, demoralizing and upsetting. You want to be valued for your hard work. It's only reasonable to hope for acknowledgement and support. Frustration in relationships can come from the same old patterns being repeated, either by you or your partner. Mostly, this happens when we don't communicate our thoughts and feelings clearly. There are some things in life that we just can't control: illness, the weather, your partner's bad moods, not to mention frustrations with society in general. It's not unusual for people to respond to frustration by giving up, but, when you know you're right, something inside you tells you to stick with it and not be beaten.

Support & guidance Look at the facts from an objective viewpoint. What is happening? Who is involved? What is your part in this drama? There's one sure rule in life and that is that we can't change others, only ourselves. If people behave in a way that pushes your buttons, learn to work on yourself, your boundaries and your expectations. Stop trying to be in control: you are the captain of your own ship, not the fleet. Rather than feeling let down by others, or unhappy at their reactions, be the best you can be, meet your own expectations, look at your goals and do things for yourself. Sail with the wind, make progress and reach your destination feeling proud and strong. Take yourself out of frustration into positive action. The road to inner peace starts with acceptance, rather than expectance.

What kind of situations frustrate you? Do you like the view you have of yourself? What changes can you make?

IMPATIENT

Definition

Having or showing a tendency to be quickly irritated or provoked. Restlessly eager.

Signs & symptoms

Huffing and puffing, talking to yourself, moaning about others and generally feeling agitated.

Impatience is that grit-your-teeth moment when you're in a rush to get somewhere and someone or something is slowing you down. If you are an impatient type, you will know that feeling of frustration, watching the slow person in the queue at the checkout packing things methodically while having a friendly chat. 'Come on – hurry up!' you think. 'I haven't got all day.' You have places to go, work to do, shopping to get, and you're on a schedule. There is no time for chatting and being leisurely in your world. 'Oh, if only I had all day, how nice that would be.' Impatience is abandoning your shopping trolley in a huff, walking out of the store and then realizing you need to do it all again somewhere else.

Support & guidance Are you generally a patient or impatient person? What kind of things make you impatient? How do you react and how do you feel afterwards? Impatience causes unnecessary stress and anxiety. Your huffing won't change things for the better and may make things worse. When you get hot under the collar, your temperature rises and so does tension in your body. As your thoughts become negative towards others – even those you don't know – that intolerance turns inwards onto yourself and you are the only one that suffers. If things aren't going quite at the speed you planned, be calm, breathe deeply, breathe again, and know that you too have all day, every day. Perhaps it's time to slow down and be more present to life and mindful of each moment, however annoying that moment may be.

How does impatience affect your life?
What stops you taking life at a slower pace?

Heart racing, mind whirling, thoughts overwhelming.

STRESS

Definition

Overwhelming physical, emotional and mental strain resulting from pressure or a threat.

Signs & symptoms

Feeling tense, anxious, confused, powerless, disengaged.

Stress is the body's normal survival response to changing demands. Major stressors are death, marriage/separation, personal injury or illness, redundancy, retirement and pregnancy (to name a few). Minor stressors could be relationship conflicts or being overloaded with looming deadlines at work. Whatever the reason, the symptoms need to be taken seriously. Stress affects us mentally (racing thoughts, constant worry, difficulty concentrating), physically (headaches, muscle pains or tension, dizziness, sleep problems) and emotionally (feeling anxious, restless, overwhelmed, fearful, depressed). When you're stressed, it's hard to think clearly and rationally, make decisions or find a way forward. Stress occurs when we are rocked from security into a situation that feels out of our control and unmanageable.

Support & guidance Understanding the trigger for any stress is the first step to overcoming it. You can't control others, nor can you control all situations – but you *can* work on your response. Perhaps you need to learn to be more assertive, or to let go of resentment. By holding on, it's only you that suffers; refocus your energy elsewhere. Some stress is good for us; it can make us stronger and more determined. Share your problems with someone you trust. Invest in some 'me' time: take up a new hobby or listen to a relaxation track; do yoga or meditate to calm mind, body and soul. Slow down and take one thing at a time. Live in the moment. Eat well and sleep well. Walk in the countryside or sit by a river. Stress will pass like the flowing water. Breathe in calm, breathe out tension. All is well.

What kind of situations stress you out?
What lessons can you learn from stressful experiences?

Free from strain and tension.

RELAXED

Definition

Free from tension, anxiety and pressure; not rigorous, strict or demanding; easy and informal in manner; not ruminating on the past or overly concerned about the future.

Signs & symptoms

Chilled out, blissful, easy to be around, worry-free, in the flow.

No worries, pressure or stress, comfortable and at peace within … What a wonderful feeling to have! Relaxed people are easy to be around because they radiate calm energy, which also helps others to let go and just *be*. Relaxation is vital for mind, body and soul. We all need it, but some find it difficult to switch off from everyday problems. That's why holidays are so beneficial – a complete break from the norm. Relaxation helps slow down heart rate, lowers blood pressure, improves digestion, helps maintain blood-sugar levels, reduces stress hormones, muscle tension and chronic pain, improves sleep and reduces anger and frustration. Being relaxed and mellow helps us cope with life's challenges.

Support & guidance If you visualize yourself in a calm space, where would you be? What would you see there and how would it feel? There are huge benefits to relaxation, but, if you find it hard, it might be time to make adjustments to your work/life balance. Put relaxation time in your diary. Here are some ideas: swim and let the water hold you; enjoy your food, savouring each mouthful; lie down on the sofa with a tub of ice cream and a good movie; try yoga and meditation; take a nature walk; listen to a relaxation tape before you go to sleep; meet a friend for a coffee and a chat; create a flowerbed; drink camomile tea; read a good book; laugh; have fun. Breathe deeply into your body, connect to the moment, hear sounds and notice colours, let go of thoughts and concerns, release negativity and tension, smile inwardly and be in the moment. Release stress and welcome serenity.

Would you describe yourself as a relaxed person?
How do you calm yourself down?

BORED

Nothing ever happens.

Definition

Tired, jaded, weary and impatient, unoccupied, lacking interest in life or current activity; loss of motivation.

Signs & symptoms

Tired and irritable, with lack of stimulation; lost zest for life; being stuck with the same old job or relationship, or have nothing much going on.

Bored people seek action or new interests but are sometimes too lazy to make change. They become *boring* people, staying in the same situations year in, year out, working for twenty-five years in a job they hate, for a pension they can just about survive on. They eat the same food every day, and read the same news again and again, watch the same TV shows about the lives of other boring people and never miss an episode in case they miss something boring. Or perhaps they find the lives of the people they watch far more interesting than theirs, although they wouldn't want to be them. Boring people stay in relationships with people they're not happy with, but wish someone far more exciting would turn up and whisk them away. But they won't leave, for fear of things being worse – a rut is a comfort zone.

Support & guidance If your life isn't exciting you any more, then perhaps it's time to make some changes. When was the last time you did something spontaneous? What do you enjoy? What are your passions? Try to find new hobbies and activities, meet up with old friends or join new groups and meet new people. Set yourself a goal or challenge that will take you out of your comfort zone. Sign up for a marathon or a fundraiser. Volunteer at a local homeless project. The world is full of opportunities that can bring a spark back into your life. Anything and everything is possible, if you come out of the boring box and set yourself free. Don't let life pass you by.

What would make your life more interesting and fulfilling?
What do you need to do?

A wonderful sense of contentment within

CONTENT

Definition

A state of peaceful happiness and acceptance; being pleased with life, satisfied with what you have and grateful for your blessings.

Signs & symptoms

Being worry-free, easily pleased, without expectations; walking round with a smile on your face for no reason.

The saying 'The best things in life are free' is so true. You can't buy love, happiness or success; so, too, with contentment. It's the small things in life that often make us the most content, such as walking in the woods and looking around in wonder at the splendour of the seasons; feeling footprints in the sand and hearing the sound of the waves lapping on the seashore; enjoying a meal with family and friends; playing with children; sitting in the sunshine reading a good book. Whatever your situation, having an attitude of contentment is likely to radiate peace within you and attract positivity into your life.

Support & guidance It's easy to get caught up in the stresses of daily living. It can feel like being on a hamster wheel with no time for rest. If you're dissatisfied with your life, think about why. Is your life working for you or against you? Think about the changes you can make to bring more joy into living. It might be about changing jobs, moving home or distancing yourself from negativity. In the meantime, start with a smile to bring positive energy into your being. It's a small step for a big result. There's no point waiting for contentment to arrive. Live in the moment, take time to smell the roses, be the best you can be, help others, do random acts of kindness, be a friend to yourself, count your blessings, accept the past and live in the present moment. Enjoy nature, music, art, books and poetry to bring a sense of relaxation and contentment within. We all have good days and bad days, but moments can always be good if we focus our minds in a positive way.

What brings you contentment?
How can you bring more joy and happiness into your life?

VICTIM

Definition

A person who's been harmed, injured or killed as a result of a crime, accident or other incident, been tricked or duped, or who's come to feel helpless and passive in the face of misfortune or ill-treatment.

Signs & symptoms

Feeling vulnerable and powerless following a traumatic incident or abuse; not feeling that you have a voice or that you can be assertive.

Being a victim of circumstance, such as being in the wrong place at the wrong time, can leave you feeling shocked, bewildered and thinking, 'Why me?' A crime against you or your property may make you feel violated and unsettled. Then there's falling victim to manipulation or trickery by someone you trust, which is much harder to recover from. You fall in love with your 'soulmate' and it's a match made in heaven, until they ask to borrow a large sum of money … This is a devastating betrayal of trust and love. Manipulative people are very good at gaining trust and knowing when to strike. This can leave a person feeling vulnerable and wary about entering into relationships or making big decisions in the future.

Support & guidance If you've been a victim of crime, give yourself time to recover, talk it through and make sense of it in your mind. Be careful not to take on the identity of victim, as this just means you're carrying the past with you. Walking around looking vulnerable, with your head down and shoulders hunched, could make you a target. Putting out negative vibes is likely to be met with negativity. If you see yourself as having a poor chance of success in life, not applying for jobs because you believe someone better will turn up, staying in an unhappy or abusive relationship because you think that's what you deserve, then you have a 'victim mentality'. Build up your confidence, become more familiar with your skills and talents, socialize, take up hobbies and be open to all that life has to offer. Don't join the pity party – focus on the positives.

Do you have a victim mentality?
What do you need to do to find strength, be assertive and in control?

I'm fine.

PASSIVE-AGGRESSIVE

Definition

Indirect expression of anger and aggression rather than honest communication of emotions. Can be very emotionally abusive.

Signs & symptoms

Knowing there is a problem but being unwilling or unable to communicate it, instead giving confusing signals that something is wrong, alongside angry body language.

Passive-aggressive people find it very difficult to express their emotions – especially anger – and, rather than honest communication, use avoidance tactics such as silent treatment. Other typical behaviours include evading problems and issues, procrastination, obstruction, being ambiguous or becoming a victim and regressing to childlike ways. Being on the receiving end can feel confusing and emotionally abusive. You may get a sense that something is very wrong but, unless your partner tells you, it will feel like you are in a limbo land of unfathomable conflict. It can result in your own passive aggression, more due to fear of further conflict. Passive aggression stems from childhood experience of not being listened to or properly valued. Overly harsh parenting teaches the child to manipulate in order to get their needs met, and this behaviour can continue into adulthood.

Support & guidance If you are passive-aggressive, what are the underlying emotions behind your behaviour? What is it you really want to say, and what stops you? Try not to feel attacked when faced with a problem, but instead take an objective view of the situation. Talk honestly about your thoughts and feelings, and make time to listen to others. There doesn't have to be a right or wrong. If you're on the receiving end of passive aggression, think about your role in this dynamic. What's behind that? Be more aware of your own responses to others and the consequences. Assertiveness is the key to building healthy relationships where both parties can speak freely and honestly without fear of conflict.

How does passive-aggressive behaviour impact on your life?
What do you need to do to improve the situation?

SAD

Definition

Feeling or showing sorrow or unhappiness; depressed.

Signs & symptoms

Tearful, unhappy, maybe even heartbroken; feeling empty, lost and low on energy.

Sadness often follows an event over which we have little or no control, such as a death, illness or seeing someone you love in pain. There is nothing harder than the pain of loss; the sadness felt when you lose someone or something special. The sadness of a relationship break-up can be similar to grief; both are painful experiences. When someone leaves you, they're making a choice not to be with you. That sadness also ties in with disappointment, rejection and abandonment. Depression can occur as a result of a stressful event, and the sadness experienced can feel deep and all-encompassing.

Support & guidance Feeling sad is a normal reaction to a life-changing event or disappointing situation. It's important to acknowledge your sadness and the reasons for it, and it's natural to want to make sense of things. Try not to blame yourself, because that will never bring you comfort. Be kind to yourself – you're hurting enough right now. You have every right to your sad times, so don't try to run away from them. Instead, take care of yourself during your darkest moments, allow the tears to fall and gently wipe them away. Comfort yourself under a big blanket and let all the emotions flow. Don't hold back. Sadness is part of being human. There's no right or wrong way to cope with it – it's about what works for you. Communicating your thoughts and feelings will help; otherwise, it all gets locked inside, where it can eat away at you and make you ill. Find solace in books, nature, music and poetry. All emotions are temporary and soon you will look back at this memory.

What has brought you sadness in the past?
What did you learn from this experience?

Open your heart to joy and your life will change forever!

JOY

Definition

A warm feeling of abundance, pleasure, peace and happiness.

Signs & symptoms

Inner contentment, appreciation of friends and family, open-hearted and grateful. Jumping for joy; tears of elation.

Joy can come from the simplest things in life. Emotional moments with loved ones or the most special occasions can bring tears of joy and happiness. We're truly blessed when we can look around us, at our friends and family, and build memories to be cherished. It's vitally important for our peace and well-being to make daily connections with the smallest of joys, such as the wonders of nature, the sun on your face. Letting yourself flow in the rhythm of sound and symphony or dance is where you'll find your inner joy and freedom. Playing is not just for children. Having fun, messing about or laughing uncontrollably at a silly joke not only increases joy and happiness, but boosts the immune system, too.

Support & guidance How many of us live life with closed hearts, defending ourselves from previous hurts? When things go wrong, our default mechanism is to be wary – to hold ourselves back, keep ourselves safe. Ultimately, we're cutting ourselves off from joy! If you feel joy is lacking in your life, consider who, or what, is stealing it. Try to surround yourself with positive, caring people, so you can feel nurtured, loved and supported. Perhaps *you* are the negative one, with regrets and doubts. Make the best of what you have, not what is lacking. Joy comes from within: what changes can you make to feel better – small or big? Make time for yourself, connect with friends. Pick up the phone – cut social media and false realities. Pay attention to the beauty of the world around you and be spontaneous. Say yes to opportunities, be grateful for your life and never let it be you that holds you back.

How often do you count your blessings?
What stops you feeling joy in your life?

INTROVERT

happy on my own

Definition

Someone who is fine in their own space but can feel drained and under pressure in high-intensity social environments. Opposite to extrovert.

Signs & symptoms

Preferring to be alone, enjoying own company, possibly socially awkward, can be misinterpreted as unfriendly, rude or unsociable.

Introverts are happy to be on their own for hours a day, and tend to avoid social gatherings. Deep thinkers, they love quiet conversations around meaningful topics but struggle when it comes to small talk. Their temperament is frequently misunderstood as shyness, social phobia or even avoidant personality disorder, but many introverts can socialize easily; they just strongly prefer not to. Introverts are hard to understand, because being outgoing and extrovert is viewed as the route to social and work success. Introvert behaviour is not a choice; it's a personality trait and lifestyle for people who like their own company and feel able to rest and rejuvenate away from crowds and noise. They are not depressed, and they definitely don't need help.

Support & guidance How does being an introvert affect your life? What are the benefits and drawbacks? If you find yourself constantly being encouraged to socialize, network and party, it might be time to claim your Introvert Identity. Let others know you're quite happy on your own; you're not shy or anxious, but just don't enjoy big gatherings. Don't make excuses for yourself. If friends love and value you, they will respect and accept you for who you are. However, if you feel you're alone too much of the time, perhaps you've said no too often and no longer get invites. Call up a close friend and arrange a coffee, lunch or day out; keep it time-contained, so you can leave when things feel too much. Being happy on your own is something many people wish for but find hard to achieve.

What's the best thing about being an introvert?
What do you most enjoy doing when you are on your own?

EXTROVERT

Definition

An outgoing, socially confident person; a people person; opposite to introvert.

Signs & symptoms

Sociable; preferring to be around others than being alone; confident; easy to talk to; looking for opportunities to shine and be the centre of attention.

Extroverts tend to seek out social stimulation and opportunities to engage with others. They are often described as being full of life, energy and positivity, but they also feel energized by others and tend to get bored by themselves. They openly communicate in social settings, where they're outgoing and vibrant (while feeding their egos). They love talking and telling stories to make others laugh – and are often seen as the life and soul of the party. Extroverts are confident and tend to build successful careers in public life, although some do like the sound of their own voice just a little too much. It can be hard to get a word in when in the company of an extrovert.

Support & guidance We are all part introvert and part extrovert, so, with a little effort, it's possible to be a bit more outgoing if you feel that it will help you in some way. The first step is to accept yourself the way you are. It is OK not to be the *most* extroverted, fun person in the room. Every actor needs an audience! However, if you want to take the stage now and again, you might need to practise your social skills. Take yourself out of your comfort zone and start new hobbies to give you something interesting to talk about. Challenge and surprise yourself at the same time. If you're an extrovert who always takes the stage, consider inviting others to join you. Give space for them to talk and develop your empathy and listening skills. A good balance of introvert and extrovert characteristics will help you to not only reach success, but keep it too.

Are you more of an extrovert or an introvert? How can you strike a healthy balance?

BATTERED

Definition

Injured by repeated blows or punishment, or having suffered repeated violence.

Signs & symptoms

Being pushed around – either physically, emotionally or verbally – and feeling unable to defend yourself, leading to feeling worn down, fearful or withdrawn, and to problems at work or in your social life. Distorted body image and views of the self.

Abuse generally isn't present at the beginning of a relationship. Initially, it might have felt loving and exciting; you probably felt safe and protected by your partner. But, gradually, their behaviour may have become more controlling, manipulative, obsessive, jealous or verbally abusive. Feeling battered is confusing and disorientating, and can leave you shocked and traumatized. If this happens over a long period of time, it can become increasingly difficult to fight, control or defend yourself, to the point where you might even blame yourself for causing it or believe that you deserve no better. Abuse, whether it occurs once or often, leaves long-lasting scars and the effects will be felt long after the injuries have healed.

Support & guidance When you're in the depths of darkness, it can be hard to see the light, and the reality of what is happening may feel too hard to bear. You can't change others; only you can make the change. If you feel that you have suffered enough, take a long hard look at the situation and make the right decision for yourself. What words best describe you both? Is one or both of you holding on for the wrong reasons? It is never too late to end an unhealthy dysfunctional relationship. If mental health issues, addiction or personality disorders are a factor, then professional support will really help. Come back to who you are, your life, your strengths and your qualities. We all deserve to live in peace and happiness and to be surrounded by positive people. Sometimes a move away, a detachment, is needed to make space for a more positive future.

When is enough enough?
What is stopping you from making change?

On Guard

WARY

Definition

Showing caution around others or in specific situations; being on guard, careful, alert to possible danger.

Signs & symptoms

Not feeling you can be yourself around certain people or speak honestly for fear of outcome; avoiding situations that might cause you harm.

We start life as trusting little souls, believing the world to be a magical place and the people in it to be caring and trustworthy. We run and jump around with confidence, as though we're invincible. As we grow up, it becomes apparent that there are dangers out there and that some people don't have our best interests at heart. When we've been hurt, used, abused or betrayed by someone we trusted, such as a parent or primary caregiver, this changes the way we view ourselves, our relationships and the world. We learn to protect and defend ourselves from hurt and harm, and being wary helps us to do this. It's our intuitive guide to keep us from danger, our emotional coat of armour that keeps us safe.

Support & guidance Being wary enables us to move cautiously and tread carefully around people or places. It also teaches us when to avoid people altogether. If you have a sense that somebody isn't right for you, then act on it. Give others a chance, but if bad behaviour is repeated, you have a choice – use it! Surround yourself with people who are genuine and bring positivity. If you're *always* on guard, this might be stopping you from having fulfilling, happy relationships in the future, because you're not giving others a chance. Be careful not to judge people on the behaviour of others in your past. Consider letting go of the past and learning to have faith in humanity again. Trust your intuition to keep you safe from harm, but be open and honest because, whatever the outcome, you will cope. You have before, so you can again.

How does being wary affect your life?
What needs to happen for you to trust again?

On edge.

What's happening?

ANXIETY

Definition

An unsettled feeling of fear, worry or nervousness (often connected to things in the past or future) that can relate to something specific or be more general.

Signs & symptoms

Fear, panic attacks, palpitations, chest pains, headaches, feeling sick, sweaty, butterflies, feeling faint, needing to go to the toilet more, worrying about the future, feeling on edge, disturbed sleep, poor concentration, irritability, change in appetite.

We all feel anxious from time to time. It's a normal part of life, especially when faced with difficult situations. It becomes a problem when it manifests into symptoms that disrupt normal everyday functioning. People get anxious for various reasons: conflict with others, fear of being assertive, work issues, fear of judgement or relationship problems. Common life events to cause anxiety are divorce/separation, bereavement, moving home, prison, marriage, health, redundancy or retirement. Anxiety can be triggered by internal worries or external stimuli, which can either be major or minor. One negative thought can quickly lead to another: 'I'm going to fail'; 'I'll get stuck in an elevator'; 'I've got cancer'; 'People will judge me …' Anxiety can be learned behaviour, but it's never too late to address the problem.

Support & guidance Cognitive behavioural therapy (CBT) can teach you to understand how your negative thinking and beliefs affect your anxiety and help you to create more beneficial thoughts. In the meantime, when you feel anxious, distract your thoughts. Go outside into the fresh air, breathe deeply, listen to calm music, dance like nobody's watching, be truly in the moment. Get creative – start a bullet journal, write down how you feel. Instead of focusing on negative thoughts, pay attention to nurturing yourself: eat a wholesome diet, cut out junk food and adopt a good sleep routine. Exercise to raise endorphin levels, lift weights to increase mental stamina. Practise gratitude, make a list of all the good things that have happened to you today. Trust in yourself to cope with life. You can do it!

How does anxiety affect your life?
What can you do to feel more calm, happy and relaxed?

Phew!
I can breathe again.

RELIEF

Definition

A relaxed feeling when a person is over the worst of a situation, or the removal of something painful.

Signs & symptoms

Breathing a big sigh; feeling relaxed, reprieved and ready to move on.

Relief comes at the end of worry, stress and anxiety about a situation. This might connect to health, a doctor's appointment or diagnosis, or perhaps to a work situation where you are under pressure to meet targets. Relationships can also be sources of anxiety, especially if conflict or disagreement is involved. You might be regretting something you've said or didn't do, and are not sure how make things right – or perhaps you are waiting for others to resolve things. Most of us to want to live happy, peaceful lives, though a small minority of us thrive on conflict and drama. Which category do you fall into: chaos or harmony? Relief brings calm, which is good for physical and mental health.

Support & guidance If you're worried or stressed, think about what can you do to sort things out. Life moves fast, children grow up and, before you know it, you will be looking back. In relationships, don't sleep on arguments; communicate, and try to resolve things as soon as possible. Does it matter who takes the first step? The important thing is to let others know you love them, and to feel loved back. Doing what's best for you will always be the right action. Breathe deeply, listen to your instinct and don't let pride get in the way. If you're in pain or worried about your health, do whatever you can to improve your current situation. Eat wholesome foods, try yoga or meditation, relax in nature and exercise in fresh air as much as possible; being active will focus your mind in a positive way. If you set yourself unrelenting standards, be kinder and focus on what's really important.

What tends to cause you anxiety?
How do you find peace and relaxation in your life?

We all feel pain from time to time, choked up, tearful and sometimes confused.

HURT

Definition

Being injured, wounded or damaged; feeling weakened or undermined.

Signs & symptoms

Feeling deeply disappointed, let down, scarred, broken, rocked and insecure.

We feel emotionally hurt when we're let down by others. This may be to do with expectations we have on people to treat us as we would them, and this hasn't happened. This might be over something seemingly minor, like not being listened to, valued or appreciated, but when it happens continuously, we begin to lose confidence in ourselves and self-doubt can set in. It's important to be honest about our thoughts and feelings, but if you don't feel heard, this is damaging to the soul. A betrayal of trust or abuse will leave deep scars within, causing confusion and leading to stress and depression. Holding feelings in exacerbates the problem, and it then becomes harder to make decisions, communicate effectively and ensure our needs are met. Feeling hurt takes energy that could be used for other things.

Support & guidance It's crucial to be aware of the hurt inside yourself and understand that you have control over your life and whether you allow yourself to be hurt again. It's hard to make change, walk away and move on, yet to allow yourself to continually be hurt is a form of self-harm. No one has to suffer at the hands of another. We all have the right to take care of ourselves, and must do so. Acknowledge the reasons for your hurt and try to talk them through with someone you trust. Think about lowering your expectations of others to avoid disappointment, or learn to be more assertive in speaking your mind. An argument or disagreement can enable both parties to air their feelings and then move on, without holding onto hurt. Hurting makes you human and can guide you for the future.

What has been your most painful hurt?
How did you move on?

SHAMELESS

Definition

A lack of shame, empathy, guilt or remorse.

Signs & symptoms

Pushing forward with your own agenda; self-serving; outrageous, with no thought for others.

No one likes to feel shame – it's painful when we face our bad behaviours. However, doing so helps to shape and motivate us to be better in the future. In shame, we view ourselves through the eyes of others, perhaps hiding from them, but also reflecting and making amends. It says heaps about who we are. The shameless among us brazenly boast about morally unsociable or unacceptable activities. They cross boundaries, manipulate, lie, take advantage of others and have a grandiose sense of entitlement with no sense of personal responsibility, letting others take the blame for their behaviour. There is no moral code or empathy. Psychopaths and sociopaths fall into this category. The shameless are barefaced and brash.

Support & guidance Can you remember times when you've behaved in a shameful way? How did you feel afterwards? Being able to face shame will help you in the future – but there is also much to learn from the shameless (while keeping your moral code). They don't worry about seeking approval, aren't concerned about other people's opinions and don't hold back on voicing their own, and seem to get what they want in life. They don't let obstacles stand in their way. Now, coming back to you … Do other people's opinions matter too much to you? Do you wait for approval before you make decisions? Do you speak your mind or hold back due to fear or lack of self-belief? Are you a go-getter or an obstacle builder? Tell it to yourself straight, be shamelessly honest, then give yourself a big cocky inward smile for your happy, successful future – which you so deserve!

Do you feel shame or are you shameless?
What is the most shameless action you have taken or witnessed?

DESPONDENT

The times when you feel stuck in a rut, BLUE, and your body energy is low.

Definition

In low spirits; loss of hope or courage; disheartened.

Signs & symptoms

Feeling that you can never get anything right; oppressed, discouraged, hopeless, sad, unhappy.

Despondency usually follows a stressful situation, an illness or a difficult period in a relationship. Perhaps you've tried, over and over again, to get a certain person to understand you and your way of thinking. Conflict is something you don't really want to engage in but that often happens when you try to speak out. Overall, you're not happy. In friendships, perhaps you're let down on a regular basis or feel left out of conversations, or maybe you find it hard to communicate. You begin to feel like you don't matter and as though you might as well not be there. At work, you are passed over for promotions and not taken seriously. When you have something to say, you just don't bother because it doesn't feel worth it; being ignored feels like a rejection every time.

Support & guidance Are things really that bad? When you feel low, it can be hard to snap out of it. Despondent moods are also moods of ingratitude, because you're focusing on what's wrong or lacking rather than on what you have. Despondency often connects to other people, and their perceived judgements or reactions to you. It's important to accept that we all have a right to our feelings and opinions and it's OK to be different. Rather than looking to others for approval, validation and acceptance, look instead to yourself for all that is positive about you. Focus on what makes you happy, what you enjoy. Nurture yourself with good food, kindness and relaxation. Surround yourself with people that ignite your soul, rather than diminish it. Be the light in your life and have hope for a happy future.

What is the cause of your despondency?
What needs to change?

EXHAUSTED

Definition

Extremely tired, having used up all energy and resources.

Signs & symptoms

Feeling completely worn out, on your last legs and ready to drop (especially likely if you're a relentless worker, a helper, or have a tendency to do things for others at the expense of yourself).

Exhaustion is the point you come to when you've run out of energy and have nothing left to give. You're ready to flop, fall asleep, hide under the covers and not come out any time soon. You can no longer concentrate, think straight or hear clearly. When your mind isn't functioning properly, this can leave you feeling confused and upset. Exhaustion is most likely to happen when you're stressed, have a huge workload that feels unmanageable, or if you've been through a major trauma, life change or illness. Maybe you've been neglecting yourself for a long time. Your body is giving you a very strong message that says rest. The mind, body and soul are all connected and need to be listened to and cared for. If you ignore the messages, you're creating future health problems for yourself.

Support & guidance The best thing you can do if you feel exhausted is *nothing*. You will know why you feel that way. No need to justify, explain or defend. You are human and there is only so far you can go. A bit like an engine without petrol, we come to a standstill when the fuel runs out. Your physical symptoms are speaking to you loud and clear. What are they saying? Rest, eat the right foods to give support, take fresh air, exercise regularly to raise endorphins and get your oomph back. Before long, your energy will flow freely and your mind will become clearer and more focused. Periods of exhaustion can be transition times to rethink your life, your path and what you want for yourself, and the steps you need to take to get there.

How hard do you find it to let go, relax and do nothing?
What needs to happen for you to feel better?

POSITIVE

I am inspired, motivated and proactive. I make the best out of every situation.

Definition

An optimistic mindset; constructive, confident; not being held back by negative beliefs or pessimism.

Signs & symptoms

Being successful, energetic, relaxed and adaptable to most situations.

Positive people see possibilities where others see obstacles. They don't dwell on what goes wrong; they learn from it and move forward in an upbeat, hopeful way. They dream big and dare to fail, because, whatever happens, they will have succeeded in trying something new and risky. Positive people are hopeful, inspired, motivated and happy. They always look on the bright side, see the best in others, turn bad situations into opportunities, love and make the most of life, enjoy meeting new people and having new experiences. Positivity is waking up to a glass that's not just half full but brimming over the top. It's an energy that reflects and extends beyond yourself. You walk down the road with a friendly smile and others smile back at you. Relationships flourish when you have a positive personality.

Support & guidance Having a positive mindset is about mental attitude and, like other skills, this can be learned. Positivity is likely to bring success and happiness into your life. If you are naturally sceptical about ideas, self-critical or tend to focus on what might go wrong, you're probably holding yourself back from reaching your full potential. Remember: what consumes your mind will influence your life decisions. You may not be able to control a situation, but you *can* control your thoughts and beliefs surrounding it. CBT helps to change the downward spiral of negative thoughts, anxiety, fear and hopelessness to more positive thoughts, happiness, relief and motivation. Negative thoughts can be switched off when you realize that they're not true or rational. Changing your way of thinking is the key to changing your life.

Are you more of a positive or negative person?
How does being positive improve your life?

INDECISIVE

Definition

Not being able to make a clear or specific decision; an indecisive person is unsure, unclear and not able to make up their mind quickly or effectively.

Signs & symptoms

Changing your mind often, taking a long time to think about choices, 'umming and ahhing', dithering, not having the confidence to decide.

Why is it that some people can make decisions quickly, while others drag their feet? It comes down to trusting yourself and your instinct, and not getting bogged down in the 'what ifs'. Quick decision makers tend to be more willing to take a chance. It doesn't mean they're not assessing the situation, but that the focus is more likely to be on moving forward rather than staying static. Future predictions of regret certainly wouldn't stop a decisive person in their tracks. If things don't turn out, there will always be another option. Life can move quickly or it can feel stuck. Nothing is permanent, and trusting yourself and your ability to accept the consequences is key.

Support & guidance When struggling to make a decision, think about the worst thing that can happen if you choose X over Y. Can you have X *and* Y – does it need to be one choice versus the other? People who are indecisive often feel that, if they make the wrong decision, they will live to regret it or it will have a negative impact on the future. Perhaps you need to be more of a risk taker and be willing to accept the results. If you are fine with the small stuff but struggle with the larger decisions in life, like moving home or changing jobs, then a good strategy to bring clarity to a situation is to make a list of the pros and cons. Think about what's really important to you and your future goals. Work towards them rather than playing it safe. You can't make an omelette without cracking eggs!

What difficult big decisions have you made in your life?
Do you trust your own instinct or look to others for advice?

LIMERENT

Definition

The state of being infatuated or obsessed with another person; agonizing love that is not reciprocated; feels crazy and out of control.

Signs & symptoms

Intrusive, compulsive and obsessive thoughts and behaviours targeted at a 'Love Object' (LO). Physical symptoms of anxiety or panic; psychological symptoms such as abandonment and despair.

Limerent love is painful when the recipient doesn't feel the same way or give much back in terms of love or kindness. They constantly disappoint and you repeatedly make excuses for them. When friends and family tell you that you need to move on, you don't listen. You stop talking honestly for fear of judgement. It doesn't make sense to you, but you can't break free. It feels like a painful addiction to a rosy image of the two of you in perfect harmony. It might feel like you're under a spell, where your thoughts lift you into pleasurable feelings of elation and ecstasy, followed by moments of despair. It's a constant replay in your head of all the things they've said or done that led to this preoccupation.

Support & guidance You may have felt good initially, but now you probably feel mostly pain and desperation. You've spent a long time trying to win your LO over, meet up with them, possibly even stalked them. Is this a one-way street? If you were your best friend, what would you say to yourself? If you're preoccupied and obsessed, you need to break the pattern before it breaks you. Try writing a series of letters to the LO (not to be sent). Write for 30 minutes at the same time every day and don't hold back. Do this for a week. When you think of them outside this time, push the thoughts away. This tactic will allow you to flood your mind to the point of saturation/boredom. You have a lot of love to give, and to free this up you need to detach and break the unhealthy attachment so your energy can flow properly once more. Only when love flows back and forth will you know your soulmate.

What evidence is there that your LO wants to be with you?
How is this obsession likely to end?

weak ... empty ... and vulnerable

beyond help

HELPLESS

Definition

*Unable to stand up for – or defend –
yourself or others; powerless, incompetent
or incapable of acting independently.*

Signs & symptoms

*Feeling weak or vulnerable; not capable
or independent enough to make a decision
or move forward in life; unaware of your
own strength; not feeling in control
of a situation.*

Feeling helpless can be a reaction to something external that has happened to you, like losing your job or being a victim of a crime or natural disaster. Having no control over an event or situation can leave you feeling powerless. Alternatively, you may feel helpless for others you care about, perhaps because of illness or bad news. They may ask for help, but you know there are limits to what you can do. Then there is 'learned helplessness' where, over a period of time (possibly since childhood), you've learned that there's no point in trying because you won't succeed. You may feel there's nothing you can do to overcome this way of thinking, which further exacerbates the problem. Being helpless can lead to secondary gains: people feel sorry for you, cook for you, give you money, take you out … They might make excuses for you, feeding your sense of helplessness in the process.

Support & guidance If you're feeling helpless, wandering through life, waiting to be rescued, advised and pointed in the right direction, do you like this view of yourself? Whatever has happened to you in the past, the future is in your hands. You can make your own decisions if you trust your instinct. Remember who you were before you felt this way. Let the flames of passion and excitement burn through you once more. Make positive connections, speak to others, be *you*, be your best friend, be the one you want to spend your future with; no one will ever be more faithful to you than yourself. Rather than waiting to be rescued, think about how much more empowered you will feel if you stop relying on others.

*Can you help yourself, or are you beyond help?
If you weren't helpless, what could you be?*

ABUSED

Definition

Being treated in a cruel, unkind and disrespectful way, either physically, mentally, emotionally or sexually.

Signs & symptoms

Feeling damaged inside, physically and emotionally worn out; marks on the body; fear of others, being timid; anxious, depressed or isolated.

Abusive behaviour is an action, by one person or more, that crosses personal boundaries and takes advantage of another person. Physical abuse includes pushing, slapping, punching and other forms of attack or torture. It is invasive and an overpowering form of senseless violence. Sexual abusers control and manipulate others who may feel powerless to stop the behaviour. Emotional abuse, such as bullying, denigration and neglect, can show no physical signs but leave painful scars. All abuse leaves deep wounds to the soul and sense of identity which are hard to heal. It affects emotional security and leads to low self-esteem, with long-lasting impacts that can affect trust in relationships for years to come.

Support & guidance No person has the right to abuse another. If you are being abused, it's important to seek help, especially if you are confused and don't know which way to turn. Being abused over a long period is soul-destroying, but your strength and personality are still there – although maybe in hiding right now. Respect yourself enough to be honest with yourself about the situation. Communicate your feelings to others, because you have a right to do so. Consider your best interests and, if necessary, remove yourself from the situation altogether. If children are involved, this is even more reason to be brave and take a stand. Learning to be more assertive and placing strong boundaries around yourself for protection will keep you safe in future. You have the law on your side, so use it! In the meantime, surround yourself with love, positivity and people who nurture your soul, not destroy it.

How does being in an abusive relationship affect you?
Who can you speak to for support and advice?

INSECURE

Definition

*Without stable base or foundation;
anxious, hesitant, worried.*

Signs & symptoms

*Not knowing what the future holds; lack
of confidence and assertiveness; anxious,
worried and hesitant about relationships
or situations; negative thinking, jealousy,
possessiveness, making assumptions about
others, feeling left out, mistrusting others,
comparing yourself to others, coming
across as needy.*

Most of us feel insecure from time to time, but, for some, insecurity is deeply embedded in their identity. Childhood experiences of trauma, rejection, abandonment, bullying or living with addiction may be responsible. People who are insecure are more likely to struggle with uncertainty and trust issues, especially in relationships, and this can lead to negative thinking, jealousy and possessiveness. Those who try too hard to please others, or have a tendency to put others down, are probably insecure at some level. Other examples of insecure behaviours include trying to be better than others, bragging, showing off and bullying – in an effort to convince themselves that they have worth.

Support & guidance For some people, security is about finances, housing and job stability. Although you may strive to stay on top of your commitments, there may be times when these are under threat, through no fault of your own. Be prepared for what you can't control and know that when one door closes another will open. If, for you, security is more about love and commitment, think about the qualities needed for your ideal relationship. When someone says they love you, do you doubt it? Does it make you suspicious? We all deserve to be happy and secure, and the first step is loving, accepting and respecting yourself. Think about the language you feed yourself – are you kind and nurturing enough? No matter how much turmoil and chaos takes place around you, there is always a place of peace, stability and safety at your core.

*What does security mean to you?
What positive thoughts help you feel strong and secure?*

SUICIDAL

Definition

Feeling deeply unhappy or depressed, to the point where you're considering taking your own life.

Signs & symptoms

Being preoccupied with thoughts about killing yourself and how to do it. Changes in personality, behaviour and appetite – mood swings, anxiety, sleep problems, isolating behaviour, negative self-talk; neglect, avoidance, self-loathing, low self-esteem.

Experiences of feeling suicidal vary from one person to another. Some typical thoughts might be that others will be better off without you, that you're useless, unlovable, unwanted or not needed – a burden to others. When you feel desperately unhappy or depressed, it's hard to see light at the end of the tunnel. Life might feel hopeless and unbearably painful. You may even feel distant from yourself and cut off from your feelings altogether; you're functioning but not properly living. It may seem that there's no point in being you, or no point in trying any more. Your thoughts may overwhelm you and it might be difficult to reach out to others for fear of upsetting them or being judged or rejected.

Support & guidance Suicidal thoughts and feelings can be very scary and overwhelming. Even if it feels hard to open up, the earlier you let someone know, the better. You're not alone. Many people think about suicide at some point in their life. Whatever has happened to make you feel this way? Think about the consequences of you no longer being alive. Who will be affected? What might you miss out on? Seek available support, but, in the meantime, stay safe and remove potential dangers, talk to a friend or distract yourself with some deep breathing. Go outdoors for fresh air and feel the sun, wind or rain against you skin. Your life has worth – don't give up on yourself.

What has led to your suicidal thoughts?
What needs to happen for you to feel better?

MOODY

Definition

Unpredictable changes of mood; sudden bouts of gloominess or sullenness.

Signs & symptoms

Being temperamental, emotional, irritable, snappy or sulky. Being happy one moment and angry the next; taking your moods out on others.

Do your moods fluctuate a lot? Do you feel like you have no control over them? Feeling moody, in this context, isn't about extreme highs and lows, the manias versus depressions that are the hallmarks of bipolar disorder, but more about your mood switching from good to bad for the smallest of annoyances and for no apparent reason, and your behaviour deteriorating. It can be brought on by hormones, health problems or things not going as planned. The upside is that, when you feel better, you can feel positive, motivated and strong. During these good moods, you get loads done and you may even get time off to enjoy yourself.

Support & guidance What is it that changes your mood, emotions and behaviour? Bad moods can be a habit, exacerbated by negative thinking. Do you think about things going wrong, bad things happening or life being unfair? Thoughts like these bring frowns, not smiles. No one wants to feel that way, or do they? Would you prefer to spend time with a happy friend or a moody one? Perhaps being a moody person is part of your identity. What is the pay-off? When you feel happy, how does life change for you? Maybe you call friends, make arrangements or take time to enjoy the simple things. Happiness grows inside as you feel more connected to the moment. Try being mindful, exercise to raise endorphin levels, but also relax when needed. Eat wholesome foods to support your mental health and well-being, and stay away from junk food and sugar. Be kind to yourself, encouraging, accepting, hopeful and optimistic. Look for the smile of sunshine through waves of clouds.

Are you a moody person?
How do your moods affect you and those around you?

LOYAL

PROTECTIVE   DEFIANT

Definition

Giving or showing firm and constant support or allegiance to a person or institution.

Signs & symptoms

Faithful, devoted, trustworthy, reliable, protective.

To be loyal is to stand by somebody's side, keep confidences, protect and defend if necessary. Loyalty can be tested time and time again, with partners, in friendships, with family and in work situations. Being consistently loyal to others helps to build trust and respect, and can help relationships develop and grow. There may be times, however, when our loyalty leads us to keep quiet about a difficult issue, rather than speak the truth, for fear of repercussions. As parents, our primary purpose is to love, care and protect our children, but if they do wrong or behave badly and you don't acknowledge it (even to yourself), then your loyalty has overtaken your accountability and responsibility. Being loyal might not always be in your or their best interest. It's important to weigh up the facts.

Support & guidance Do you see yourself as loyal and trustworthy? Who are you loyal to, and why? Perhaps there are times when your loyalty is challenged. The most important thing is to be true to yourself and your beliefs. If you find yourself being caught up in something that doesn't feel right, be honest with yourself and follow your instinct. Being loyal to others is important in building trust and vital for strong relationships, but there can be conditions attached. Do you expect others to be loyal to you and then perhaps get disappointed when things go wrong? Perhaps you are too protective, even protecting people from themselves. This prevents them from learning how to take responsibility for their actions. Good communication is key to avoiding any potential conflict or misunderstandings in the future.

What does loyalty mean to you?
In what circumstances would your loyalty be tested?

OVERWHELMED

Definition

Overcome with emotion, overloaded, flooded, weighed down.

Signs & symptoms

Feeling buried or drowning in tasks or emotions, to the point where it feels hard to handle and difficult to think straight.

Whether it's a result of joy or grief, we feel overwhelmed when an event or situation touches us deeply on an emotional level – the effects can be more extreme if we're already run-down or vulnerable. Being overwhelmed can be a really positive feeling, such as excitement, joy and happiness at the birth of a new baby or a very special occasion such as a wedding, where you look around you and see the emotions of others reflected back at you. On the other hand, it can be a feeling of devastation if you lose someone you love. Grief is overwhelming and destabilizing. Whatever you think and feel at this time is valid. If your situation is self-inflicted, you're probably putting undue pressure on yourself to reach and achieve your goals. Are you taking on too much work, or doing too much people-pleasing? Think about the cost to your health.

Support & guidance In whatever way you're feeling overwhelmed, and whatever the reasons, you can be reassured that this feeling will pass. Take your time. There is no rush! Perhaps you have unrelenting standards and never stop to smell the roses … What is it that drives you? At what point would you take your foot off the pedal? If you're being overloaded with work, learn to say no. It's OK to look after yourself. If you're the cause of your own emotional download, then take stock of what's important and be a friend to yourself, put boundaries in place to protect yourself and cut yourself some slack. Be assertive where necessary. There is only one you!

What kind of situations overwhelm you?
How can you make powerful positive changes for yourself?

NEGATIVE

Definition

A mindset that creates obstacles to moving forward; lacking positive or affirmative qualities, such as enthusiasm, interest or optimism.

Signs & symptoms

Frustrated, pessimistic, down, hard to please or impress; displaying a lack of confidence, distrust, anxiety; constantly worrying. Someone who is all 'doom and gloom'.

Negative people think the worst of any situation, especially if they're also prone to anxiety. If one thing goes wrong, it can be the catalyst to a downward spiral of unhelpful thoughts and feelings. It's never the event itself that's the problem, but the way you think about it. Typical thoughts of a negative person might be: 'I'll fail'; 'Nobody likes me'; 'Everything I do goes wrong'; 'I can't do this'; 'I'm stupid, a bad person, worthless!' Negative thinkers are often habitually down on themselves, with low self-esteem and confidence. Life doesn't always turn out the way we want it to. While a positive person will move ahead and not ruminate or get stuck in time, a negative person might hold onto resentments, arguments or perceived personal failures and be more self-critical. It's all about mindset!

Support & guidance Is your glass half full, or half empty? Is it easier to notice the things you do wrong, or what you do right? If you've always been a moaner, downer and doubter, that may be the character that's become you. 'Black hat' thinkers don't take as many opportunities as others. What have you missed out on by being too hard on yourself or too worried about what could go wrong? Reprogramme your mental attitude. Rather than thinking 'I'm no good at anything', try 'I'm a good driver and a good cook'. CBT can teach you to change your thinking and change your life. Make a pledge to yourself to no longer allow negative thoughts to drain you of your energy. Instead, set your mind to focusing on all that's good about you and let positive energy flow through you and out into the world.

In how many ways does your negative thinking hold you back? What are you good at? What have you achieved?

Pleased with myself.
I smile inwardly.

SATISFIED

Definition

*Content and pleased with something
or someone.*

Signs & symptoms

*Feeling pleased, proud, triumphant,
smug, happy and grateful.*

When you can sit back and relax with a smile on your face, that is satisfaction. You know in your heart and mind that you've done a good job, worked hard, said the right thing, stepped up to a challenge and tried your best. It's wonderful when we're able to tell ourselves that we can be satisfied; we value our work and our efforts and are kind to ourselves about our achievements. We acknowledge our successes and don't wait for validation from others. Of course, any positive feedback can confirm our thoughts, but it isn't essential. You might feel that it's time to treat yourself, have a break, watch a movie, go out for a nice meal and celebrate. We all need downtime, to re-energize, rest and recuperate. If you've just come to the end of a big project, you might even want to take a well-deserved holiday.

Support & guidance What stops you from being satisfied? Often, dissatisfaction comes from having high expectations of others that are not met, or unrealistic expectations of yourself to do more, achieve more, earn more money, be more successful … We can't change others, only ourselves. If there's something you can do to make a change that will bring a greater sense of satisfaction, then do it! Satisfied people tend to appreciate themselves and their own efforts and feel grateful for the simple things in life, like home-cooked food and good friends. Seeking more on a material level won't guarantee you more satisfaction. In fact, the mere act of not being satisfied leaves you restless and seeking. Be satisfied, be grateful, be happy and be content.

*Are you generally a satisfied person or a dissatisfied person?
What needs to change for you to be satisfied with yourself?*

SELF-DOUBT

Definition

*Lack of confidence in yourself
and your abilities.*

Signs & symptoms

*Not trusting yourself to make decisions;
negative self-talk and beliefs; seeking out
or, conversely, avoiding situations that
may confirm your negative beliefs.*

Self-doubt can start to creep into the mind from a very young age. When a child is brought up with unconditional love, they're taught that it's OK to make mistakes, to know they're equal to others and should be valued. But some parents try *so* hard to get it right that they put undue pressure on their children. Discipline and boundaries are vitally important for a child to feel safe and secure; however, when the discipline is too harsh, critical or unloving, the child blames themselves and feels unworthy, creating negative core beliefs. As adults, these manifest as negative opinions about skills, body image, self-worth, and so on. Self-doubt arises when you feed yourself negative thoughts that spin out of control. Any negative events, such as redundancy, can confirm the core belief that you're not good enough.

Support & guidance Try to look at yourself with a fresh pair of eyes, to see that you're a special and worthy person. Be amazed at how strong, brave and smart you are. Hang around with your childhood self to see how awesome, pure and innocent you were. Shatter your limited view of what you can do and what you can achieve. Say no to put-downs and yes to puff-ups. How do your friends describe you? Accept praise with thanks. Don't let rejection in, don't listen to the script from the past, change the mantra – you *are* enough, no matter where you came from, where you lived, how you were treated. Try repeating positive affirmations about yourself: *'I am Enough, I am Valued, I am Strong.'* Your mind will believe everything you say – good or bad. Tell it you can succeed, and you will.

How does self-doubt hold you back?
What are your skills, talents and personal qualities?

I am who I am. Comfortable in my own skin.

CONFIDENT

Definition

Feeling self-assured; having trust in yourself, another or a situation.

Signs & symptoms

Being comfortable in your own skin and your identity; approaching situations calmly; having belief in your ability and decision-making, and trusting in the outcomes.

Confident people don't spend time worrying about being liked or judged. They act naturally, speak clearly and assertively and have no problem with others seeing things differently. They act in accordance with their morals and values but may step outside them from time to time, in acts of spontaneity or creativity. Having confidence in yourself gives off an air of calm energy and wisdom that draws others to you. It's not so much about being loud and outgoing (a quiet introvert can still be confident), but more about being clear and self-assured. There's much to learn from a confident person. A lack of confidence can lead to holding onto negative experiences or negative comments made by others.

Support & guidance People can display confidence in many areas of life – at work, in sport, in relationships, as parents … If you lack confidence, remind yourself of all that you've achieved so far in life and what it took for you to get there. Criticism shrinks you; praise puffs you up. Believe in yourself and your abilities by acknowledging and accepting yourself fully, and be kind to yourself if you make a mistake. Rather than trying to please others or putting on a mask, speak your mind – you have a right to your opinions. When something goes wrong, move forward rather than dwelling on it and analysing what's happened. There's no such thing as failure; only learning opportunities. If you need to increase your confidence in certain areas of your life, practise, practise and practise. Initial awkwardness will soon turn into automatic response – like riding a bike or driving a car.

What are you confident about?
How can you increase your confidence?

LOST

Definition

Unable to find your way; at a loss to understand or cope with a situation.

Signs & symptoms

Feeling empty, as though you have no direction in life or no control of your future.

There are times in life when we feel lost, directionless and confused about which way to turn. Often, this comes as a result of unexpected change such as redundancy, bereavement or a break-up. When you lose someone or something that has been a major part of your life, it's natural to feel sad and disorientated. You're in a place of transition, a state that sits between past and future which can feel very upsetting and destabilizing. Losing a loved one can also make us feel like we've lost our role, our identity, our purpose, our daily routine and possibly social groups. You're no longer a couple and, if you saw your partner as your 'other half', then part of you is missing. Healing takes time and this process is unavoidable.

Support & guidance When life changes unexpectedly, you may feel worried and unsure about your future. On the other hand, it could be just the moment you were waiting for to make a positive life change. Grief and mourning is inevitable. Perhaps you don't know who you are any more, or where you're going. Once you've recovered from the initial loss, you can think about what it is you really want. Transition periods open up new paths of possibility. One door closes and three more may open. Don't be alone in your loss. Talk to people, share your feelings, your hopes, your dreams and your experience. People are naturally kind and helpful at these times. Nobody is alone in this world and we can all help each other through challenging times. Don't hide behind yourself, because you won't see where you're going, and remember: your present situation is not your final destination.

Can you remember a time when you felt lost in life?
What advice would you offer to others going through this?

I feel it too.
We are so connected!

EMPATHY

Definition

Highly sensitive to energies and emotional states of others. Some empaths are also psychic, sensing the past, present and future states of others.

Signs & symptoms

Feeling touched in a physical and emotional way by someone else's story or situation. Unexplainable irrational feelings of connection or love.

Empaths are highly receptive to the emotions and energetic patterns of others – like being on the same radio frequency. An empath naturally tunes into what others are feeling or going through because they feel it too. This might be someone close to you or it could be a complete stranger. It can happen when you are in close proximity or a thousand miles away. It's like an energetic thread that flows between people, creating a drive to respond in an emotionally appropriate way. Being empathic can be a gift or a burden, depending on how you use it. Empaths pick up on energies, auras, psychic threads and spiritual imprints, which can feel hard to handle around depression, addiction or illness, often resulting in the empath feeling depleted and overwhelmed. Empaths are generally deep thinkers, spiritually connected, intuitive and often clairsentient.

Support & guidance When empathy is recognized and managed properly, it can be used as a powerful tool for healing. People are drawn like magnets to empaths because they feel heard and understood. Empaths need to have strong boundaries of protection in place, as others draw their light and positivity. Set up a daily meditation/visualization practice that involves grounding, clearing and shielding your energetic body and auric field. This will keep you clear and positive and help define your feelings from those of others. Self-care is vital, including good nutrition and exercise to raise your own energetic signals. Empathic people generally seek to live in harmony, and bring positive energy to those around them.

How does being empathic affect your life?
How do you protect yourself from unwanted energies?

No defences

VULNERABLE

Definition

Feeling exposed, unprotected, unguarded and at risk.

Signs & symptoms

Worrying about something going wrong, feeling out of control; fear of being taken advantage of or being manipulated in some way; not feeling strong enough or good enough to protect yourself – staying under the radar to stay safe.

Being unwell or mentally or physically challenged can make you feel vulnerable to danger, but vulnerability also connects to fear of others seeing who you truly are and what you truly feel. At the core of this is low self-esteem, shame and a struggle for respect. People feel vulnerable in unfamiliar settings, or when they're forced into the spotlight, such as having to do a work presentation. Vulnerability doesn't make you weak and helpless; on the contrary, it helps you to find your strength. Being out of your comfort zone can be scary and challenging, but it can also help you to be more creative and spontaneous. Being vulnerable is part of being alive, but it's an emotion we try to hide. However, showing vulnerability invites meaningful connection and empathy with others.

Support & guidance Overcoming vulnerability is about facing our fears, worries and insecurities, the internal voice of mistrust – of the self and others. We can never be certain of outcomes, so we might use vulnerability as an excuse to avoid actions that could bring up difficult emotions. If we've trusted others in the past and have been let down or attacked, it leaves a hole in our protective shell and can take a long time before we have faith again and feel strong. What makes you vulnerable also makes you human. To feel true love, joy and connection, it's important to be honest with yourself and others – to let them in – because they're vulnerable too. Nothing can hurt you more than the sound of your own criticism. Practise gratitude and joy. You are enough! Be kinder and more compassionate to yourself.

Do you try to hide your vulnerability?
What do you think will happen if you show it?

BRAVE

Definition

*Bold, courageous, resilient, daring
and adventurous.*

Signs & symptoms

*Showing no fear in the face of danger, or
putting a brave face on a difficult situation;
standing up for what is right.*

Bravery isn't always a choice, but we can choose to be brave in difficult situations. We are brave when we face our own battles with a positive attitude, such as fighting illness and not allowing ourselves to succumb to defeat, weakness or negative mental attitude. Soldiers are brave in their pursuit of loyalty and duty, fighting for a cause or putting themselves in danger to save a comrade. Sometimes bravery is forced upon us. We are put into situations where we act without thinking, without time to show true feelings or let our guard down. In life-or-death situations, we act without fear or thought for ourselves, to help another person, rescue or save from disaster. If we undertake a dangerous sport, such as motor racing or mountaineering, is that bravery or taking measured risks?

Support & guidance Bravery is overcoming your fear for the good of yourself or another. It requires courage, resilience, strength, selflessness and decision-making. We all have the ability to be brave, and can surprise ourselves when we least expect it. How brave do you see yourself? Would you like to have more courage and strength, to stand up and speak out for what is right, and be a powerful force for good? Gather strength from adversity and have strong powerful thoughts, even if you feel weak inside. Sometimes, being brave is about making big life-changing decisions. This requires a willingness to step out of your comfort zone and take a risk or two, moving through the fear barrier – and beyond. Give yourself positive thoughts and affirmations, such as 'I can do this', 'I will do that', 'All will be well'.

*What acts of bravery have inspired you?
What do you think it takes to be brave?*

worst case of
EVERYTHING

HYPOCHONDRIAC

Definition

Severe anxiety where a person is abnormally and overly anxious about their health; can be compulsive and obsessive.

Signs & symptoms

Worrying about every lump or bump, nosebleed or backache and imagining serious life-threatening diseases; incessant talk of illnesses, often seeking reassurance from others.

Hypochondriacs are consistently anxious about their health and quick to spot any sign that could potentially be something serious. Be it a headache or runny nose, there will be a dread, fear and suspicion that these are the first signs of something far more sinister, long term or incurable. After the initial anxiety and fear comes the checking and rechecking for symptoms worsening or changing into a more chronic condition. Looking online – especially on medical websites and forums – is a popular pastime; there might also be frequent visits to doctors and numerous tests to confirm the situation. However, test results are not trusted: they could be wrong or the doctor might be lying to protect you from the worst. The condition can be worse if the sufferer is reaching an age at which a parent died.

Support & guidance If much of your time and energy is taken up worrying about your health or seeking signs of illness, find out about CBT to help check your thoughts, feelings, beliefs and behaviours. You could also keep a diary and make a note of how many times you check yourself in a day. Try to reduce the anxiety by replacing unhelpful checking behaviours with distractions such as walking, exercise, singing or calling a friend. Try meditation, mindfulness or yoga to bring peace and calm into your being. Hypnotherapy can also help to break habits and loops of negativity. Imagine a flower that you feed with anxious messages; watch it grow bigger and bigger as you water it. Now imagine what would happen to that flower if you didn't feed it or give it water or sunlight.

Are you sick of anxiety about your health?
What could life be like without your anxiety?

MEDITATIVE

Definition

Absorbed in meditation, mindfulness practice; finding inner peace and well-being.

Signs & symptoms

Relaxed, in the present moment, in silence, in stillness; heightened senses.

There are lots of ways to meditate. The main purpose is to reduce stress and unwanted tension and bring relaxation, calmness, clarity and self-acceptance to mind and body. It's hugely beneficial for mental and physical health, and a good regime will bring healing and peace of mind. Meditation is rooted in Eastern philosophy and traditions that go back hundreds of years. From the Buddhists and Hindus we learn mindfulness and Zen; from India we have kundalini yoga and transcendentalism; and from China, qi gong. Meditation can take place sitting down, lying down or combined with physical activity to strengthen. You can walk it, breathe it, chant it (mantras and bhajans) or repeat affirmations.

Support & guidance Anyone can meditate. It's a way to feel better. Start with mindfulness: it's about being in the flow of the breath and aware of the present moment. Notice your breathing, body movement and changes, connect to the flow of your own rhythm, accept tension or pain, be aware of feelings that arise within you, observing, releasing unwanted stress, connecting to your surroundings. Or, breathe in to the count of 1, breathe out to the count of 1, breathe in for 2, out for 2, up to 10, and then start again. You *can* do it. Why not find a podcast or app to help you? There are so many practitioners and yoga classes that there really is no excuse not to start the process. Wherever and however you meditate, allow yourself to fully engage and embrace the experience. You will feel better, calmer and even enlightened along the way.

Do you meditate?
How do you think you would benefit from meditation?

BORDERLINE (BPD)

Definition

A personality disorder involving emotional instability, which has varying causes and symptoms making it an ongoing struggle to manage emotions and behaviour.

Signs & symptoms

Feeling happy and friendly one minute, and being upset and accusing the next; difficulty holding onto relationships due to unpredictability; feeling broken, faulty, wrong, bad and worthless, and that life is an ongoing struggle.

Borderline personality disorder is extremely challenging for those who suffer from it and hard for others to understand. It involves confidence and self-esteem issues, anxiety and depression, and feelings of emptiness, loneliness and isolation. There is a real fear of abandonment by others, which often arises from the explosive chaos and conflict in personal relationships – it becomes a self-fulfilling prophecy. Sufferers can self-harm and threaten suicide to avoid being abandoned, or self-medicate with drugs or alcohol to numb extreme internal pain. It may be caused by childhood experiences of fear, abuse, neglect or loss (though can be genetic) and exacerbated by stress, anxiety and hormone imbalances.

Support & guidance We can all be both good and bad – it's called being human. If your life is a struggle because of BPD, seek professional help such as DBT (dialectical behaviour therapy – designed specifically for BPD) or MBCT (mindfulness-based cognitive therapy). It can be hard to access mental health services, but don't give up trying. In the meantime, be with people who love and accept you, see the good in you, are grateful to have you in their lives, inspire you and are happy for you when you do well. Share your thoughts (however intense) rather than letting them build and burst. Be kind to yourself, walk barefoot on the earth, bask in the sun, sing from the heart of your soul, have fun, be weird, be wonderful. Mindfulness is excellent for calming anxious thoughts. A bad day doesn't mean a bad life. Life is an uphill journey, with stops and detours. Your internal sat nav will guide you.

How do you manage difficult emotions?
What do you love about your personality?

DETERMINED

Decision made, mind set.

Definition

Making a firm decision and resolving not to change it; focusing on the goal/objective.

Signs & symptoms

Insistent, committed, passionate, motivated, adamant, firm, undaunted.

Determination is the driver of success. When you're moving on a path that overcomes obstacles, nothing can stop you reaching your goal. Everything can be worked on, around and adjusted – avoidance is not on the agenda. Determined people do what it takes to get results. They start early, work to deadlines and plans and are strict and structured with time management. The strengths connected to determination are positive thinking, confidence, motivation, self-belief, organizational skills and communication skills. Holding a vision in the mind is vital, as without a destination, which way do you go? A clear view of an outcome helps us to be determined.

Support & guidance Who, or what, do you think determines your future? Perhaps you want to succeed with work, career, exams, relationships, friendships or financial milestones such as saving for a property or car. All of these require resolve and resilience, and that needs to come from you. Being determined does not mean everything will go exactly the way you want it to – that is life, and there might be lots of detours and changes along the way. Successful people do not see obstacles; instead, they see challenges. There is no such thing as failure, just learning opportunities. When things go wrong, make them go right. Pick yourself up and start again. Be flexible and willing to see new opportunities. Be strong, be clear, be determined and find your success.

What are you determined to achieve?
What steps do you need to take to get there?

NARCISSIST

Definition

Having, or showing, an excessive interest in or admiration of the self. Narcissistic personality disorder (NPD) involves having an exaggerated sense of one's own importance, a deep need for admiration and a lack of empathy for others.

Signs & symptoms

Everything revolves around the self; the individual sees themselves as bigger, better, stronger, smarter, more important than anyone else — a legend in their own mind.

There's nothing wrong with healthy self-love — valuing yourself and striving to fulfil your own needs. But, at its worst, narcissism is a personality disorder involving specific pervasive patterns of behaviours and character traits — a grandiose sense of self-importance, being preoccupied with fantasies of unlimited power and success, belief in being unique and deserving of special treatment. Narcissists have a very strong sense of entitlement and can take advantage of others in order to advance their own goals. They can be arrogant and pompous, with a lack of empathy and understanding for others' feelings, motives or actions.

Support & guidance If you're in a relationship with a narcissist, you probably feel isolated and unloved because full attention will never be on you. It's hard to have a meaningful connection or raise concerns, as this may be seen as an attack, which is likely to result in a barrage of vitriolic accusations and twisted tales of truth (gaslighting). Consider how this behaviour is affecting your life and what you want to do about it. Take responsibility and put clear boundaries around yourself for emotional protection. The key to understanding narcissism is knowing that, deep down, the person feels like nothing, so they put up a facade of superiority just to get through life. A narcissist will rarely say sorry, and focus instead on all the things you've done to cause the problem, which can leave you feeling confused, upset and emotionally battered. The antidote is to be sure of who you are and not be drawn into the conflict. Love your narcissist for who they are, but don't expect them to change.

How does narcissism affect your life?
What changes need to happen?

Anxious and uneasy ... Scared and concerned ...

WORRIED

Definition

Anxious or troubled about genuine or potential problems.

Signs & symptoms

Feeling concerned, stressed and preoccupied with the future.

Worries can be broken down into two types: rational and irrational. Some people are born worriers and will always have something to worry about – health, family, finances, the future … These are natural concerns, but if your worries take up too much time and space in your head, this can be exhausting. Then there are more specific worries which involve fears or phobias: flying, contamination, spiders, elevators. These irrational worries are about worst-case scenarios, where your mind can run away with itself, creating disasters in seconds. Worrying about yourself is quite different, and is more connected to self-esteem and confidence. 'Am I slim/pretty/clever enough?' Worrying affects relationships and can lead to us dreading being in a social setting or having to perform, and this limits our potential.

Support & guidance When we worry, we're giving ourselves negative thoughts and believing them. If you're a persistent worrier and want to break the habit, learn to recognize your negative thinking for what it is – thinking! A thought can't hurt you. It has no power. What, specifically, do you worry about? Can you do anything about it? Break down each thought into manageable pieces. If there's a real issue to resolve, communicate with the right person and share the problem. CBT is a great way to learn to reprogramme your mind to think more positively. Alternatively, practise yoga and meditation to calm mind and body. It's quite possible to change this habit. Learning mindfulness is a great way to connect to the present moment, where you may find there's nothing to be immediately concerned about.

How much of the day do you spend worrying?
How does worrying affect your life? What else could you be doing instead?

swinging from the chandeliers

hiding under the covers

BIPOLAR (BD)

Definition

A mental health problem that affects mood; relates to emotional extremities – manic or hypomanic (highs) and depressive (lows) – or somewhere in between (mixed states); can include psychotic symptoms.

Signs & symptoms

Having extreme mood states or switching between them; swinging from wild, chaotic behaviour to feelings of shame, depression and confusion.

We all feel up and down sometimes, but for people with bipolar disorder this can be very distressing and overwhelming. In the manic state, you might feel uncontrollably excited and easily distracted – too many thoughts racing around to focus. With increased energy, drive and confidence you will feel invincible; this can lead to inappropriate, risky behaviour that is out of character. Afterwards you may feel ashamed, perhaps not remembering what's happened. When you're low, you might experience intense emotional pain, guilt, worthlessness and hopelessness, or even have thoughts of self-harming or suicide, withdrawing from others, eating less and having disrupted sleep patterns. Mixed states include all of the above simultaneously, and it becomes a challenge to work yourself out.

Support & guidance Don't be seduced by the highs and lows. Get to understand your moods by keeping a mood diary. Look at patterns to identify the triggers preceding extreme feelings. How's your diet/drinking/sleep/exercise? Be aware of stressful situations, and make changes where necessary. Routine is good for stability. When you're active, your mood will lift, achievement will feel good and so will relaxation. Try mindfulness to help you feel calm and self-accepting. Build a support network around you. Speak honestly to trusted friends or family about how they can help you. It can be hard being around someone with BD, especially if you are sensitive too, but love and strong boundaries are a great help. We all live unique lives, so try not to judge. Be kind and compassionate – to yourself and others!

What strategies do you have to manage your moods?
How can your mood swings help you reach your potential?

DRAINED

Definition

Depleted of strength, energy and vitality, perhaps as a result of illness, working too much, too little sleep or too many worries on your shoulders.

Signs & symptoms

Feeling exhausted, physically, mentally, emotionally and spiritually; shaking through lack of energy.

Do you feel drained by work? Perhaps you feel you can never catch up with your workload, or that your targets are unrealistic. People working in public service for low income often feel demoralized and undervalued, leaving them exhausted and unable to see a way forward. People in the caring professions also have a tendency to become drained, because they're giving so much of their personal energy and strength to others. In a relationship, if you feel drained by your partner, it could be that you're giving too much and your needs aren't being met in return. This happens in co-dependent relationships, where you're constantly trying to fix or please. All energy is taken up with your partner's problems, addiction or depression. Your own life is put on the back-burner, and it slowly evaporates in the process.

Support & guidance If you're feeling physically and mentally drained, your body is giving you a very strong message – enough is enough! If you're not happy with your situation, do something about it before you make yourself ill. Think about who is putting the pressure on you. If it's other people, learn to be more assertive in saying no. You have a right to speak up for yourself if something isn't working for you. If you're loading the pressure on yourself, take a long look in the mirror to see how you'll be in one year's time if you don't make some positive lifestyle changes. Maybe you expect a lot from yourself. Are your high standards giving you the results you desire? Once away from the situation that's draining you, you can recuperate, recharge your batteries and move on to a more positive place.

Why are you feeling drained?
What changes need to happen for you to feel better?

Left out again,
alone in the cold

EXCLUDED

Definition

Denied access to a place, group or privilege, or not being considered eligible; a sense that something is going on that you're being left out of.

Signs & symptoms

Feeling rejected, left out, without company, lonely, confused, having negative self-belief or assumptions.

Being excluded can be very upsetting, and can be a form of bullying when it's intentional. Exclusion can happen in a variety of settings, for numerous reasons. At work, meetings may take place that you're not invited to, even though the content is relevant to you; or, you might feel ignored or talked over, even when you try to participate in a useful way. This can lead to a sense of exclusion from the team and leave you feeling confused and demotivated. Perhaps your best friend no longer calls you and is making arrangements with other people. Or, your partner has stopped sharing their thoughts with you. There is something going on but you don't know what – you want to be closer, but you are drifting apart.

Support & guidance If you're feeling left out, investigate by communicating your concerns in a clear, assertive way. Ask if there is a problem that you need to be aware of, or anything you can do to improve things. The answer you get may not be what you are expecting or want to hear. Be self-reflective and take responsibility where necessary. If you don't get a proper response, or an opportunity to make things better, take it as a sign that perhaps it's time to move on; look elsewhere for positive, nurturing relationships where you can thrive, grow and connect to more like-minded people. However, if you're feeling bullied, it needs to be taken seriously, so seek proper support and guidance. Make choices for yourself that serve you well. We're not all for everyone. That's life. The important thing is that you find your happiness with your tribe, whoever they are.

*Do you exclude others, or are you the one that sometimes feels excluded?
What can you learn from this?*

I am important.

VALUED

Definition

Considered to be important or beneficial; cherished.

Signs & symptoms

Feeling appreciated or thought well of; being respected and held in high regard.

Value systems are either internal or external: how we see ourselves versus how others see us (or how we think they see us). We might like to be valued for being helpful, kind, thoughtful, doing a good deed and so on, but how do we feel when we're not appreciated or our behaviour isn't reciprocated? When we're listened to, respected, heard properly and empathized with, we feel valued, real, that we can be ourselves. However, if that doesn't happen, it doesn't mean we're being judged or not cared for. Negative assumptions can lead to self-deprecation and low self-esteem. A strong sense of self will come from awareness of all your good qualities, skills and actions. Appreciate and value yourself to increase your self-esteem and positive energy. What we put out into the world will be reflected back at us.

Support & guidance Value others as you wish to be valued. Do you judge and criticize yourself, or are you accepting and forgiving of your actions? How we value others can also affect how we see and take care of ourselves. Excessive drinking, smoking, drug-taking and other unhelpful habits aren't honouring you or your body. Be mindful of positive lifestyle choices. Think about what's important to you, what you value most in life: happiness or possessions; being out in nature or going on a spending spree; a good home-cooked meal or eating out. Is it more important for someone to be kind and caring or rich and successful? There's no right or wrong answer here; it's more about understanding your own value system and assessing whether it works for you and fits with your morals and lifestyle.

Do you accept others unconditionally, or do you judge and criticize? How can you be more accepting of yourself and others?

SELF-HARM

Definition

Hurting yourself on purpose to bring relief from painful emotions.

Signs & symptoms

Cutting, burning or picking yourself to draw blood; addictive behaviours and compulsive acts that injure or destroy the mind, body and soul; feeling stressed, anxious or depressed.

People who self-harm tend to find it hard to express how they feel, perhaps due to fear of being judged or rejected, or feelings of shame. Behaviours that harm the body also harm the mind, and can easily become compulsive and uncontrollable. Negative obsessive thinking can also accompany these behaviours: for example, 'If I don't cut myself, I can't go out.' The effects of self-harm are often hidden under clothing, which ties in with feelings of shame and self-loathing. The act of self-harm brings temporary relief and can feel satisfying, even cleansing. Eating disorders and drug or alcohol addiction are self-harming behaviours that reinforce the sufferer's feeling they're not worthy of a 'normal' life. The same can be said of staying in an abusive or unhealthy relationship – self-esteem has a part to play in self-harm.

Support & guidance If you're self-harming, you probably feel sad, hurt and very alone with your thoughts and feelings. Is there anyone you can talk to? Perhaps you feel no one wants to listen to you, be there for you or can ever fully understand you. Being alone with yourself can feel empty and hopeless, and self-harming helps you to manage the hurt and feel alive – your companion in misery. Please know there are people who will be there for you, listen to you and help you express your thoughts and feelings. No, they won't fully understand your pain, but they can help you make sense of it. Verbalizing emotions takes them outside of you, which will be a relief and a weight off your mind. Seek professional help to release all the emotions that are hurting you. Don't let the scars that define you bind you.

What is it that you want to express?
What needs to happen for you to feel better?

Breathing deeply into my body

CALM

Definition

An internal state of peace, serenity and tranquillity; keeping the mind free of agitation, excitement or disturbance.

Signs & symptoms

Feeling relaxed about life; not allowing problems to take you away from your internal peace.

Some people seem to naturally be more calm than others. They don't get flustered by life, they stay steady and in the flow of the moment, rather than overreacting to situations. Calm people tend to observe life in a detached way. They still experience, but there is more of an awareness of what is happening and an ability to assess without becoming drawn into worry or anxiety. To be calm is to be in control of mind and body. Meditation and mindfulness teach you to control thinking rather than letting it control you. The drama you create from situations is just thoughts in your head – what you tell yourself might happen if X, Y or Z occurs. Peace of mind creates calmness within. Being in nature or by the sea can help to wash away worries or let them absorb into the earth.

Support & guidance Life doesn't always flow the way we expect it to, and it's important to accept the normality of life itself. It's what we're here for – to learn, to take forward, to help us grow. When thinking creates dramas in our minds, our bodies believe us. It's important to master your thinking in order to create a lifelong pattern of acceptance and living in the moment. If you find it hard to be calm, try yoga, meditation and mindfulness, which all help to bring peace and harmony within. Situations change and feelings come and go. The universe supports us to survive hard times, so don't sweat the small stuff – close your eyes, and let negative thoughts drift downstream into a deep blue ocean. Let peace flow through you and beyond you.

What are the benefits of being calm?
What can you do to bring more peace and serenity into your life?

OCD

Definition

Obsessive-compulsive disorder (OCD) is an anxiety-related condition where a person experiences frequent intrusive and unwelcome obsessional thoughts, often followed by repetitive compulsions, impulses or urges.

Signs & symptoms

Needing to perform rituals such as hand-washing or checking locks on doors, or experiencing unwanted intrusive thoughts.

OCD is unique to the sufferer but tends to fall into two main categories: persistent and uncontrollable involuntary thoughts, and compulsions in the form of repetitive behaviours and actions or mental thought rituals. It's highly disruptive to normal life and causes anguish and severe stress and anxiety. The term is also used to describe people who are overly fussy or rigid. Typical manifestations are: *checking* – doors, locks, appliances, switches; *washing* (for fear of contamination) – hand-washing, excessive cleaning; *hoarding* (for fear of letting go) – books, magazines; *self-doubting* – a need for perfection to avoid something terrible; *counting* – arranging things in certain ways, avoiding cracks in the pavement (superstition).

Support & guidance OCD is a vicious cycle of thinking, anxiety, compulsive behaviour and relief – the bully in your head! If your brain is stuck in a loop, try the following ideas. Resist the rituals by facing your fears and exposing yourself to the triggers; for example, if your fear is germs, try walking barefoot on the earth, little by little. When you see that you haven't died or been rushed to hospital, this will break the belief that has been part of your OCD cycle of washing and cleaning. Focus your attention away from negative thoughts or urges by taking exercise, walking, reading or engaging in a positive activity for at least 20 minutes. Then check the thought. Is it as powerful as before? Probably not. Write down obsessive thoughts and worries whenever you have them. Learn to challenge them. Gain control to reduce the power of the thought. Obsess in small time slots. Have an OCD hour – not an OCD life!

How does OCD affect your life?
If you didn't have OCD, how could your life improve?

MINDFUL

Aware of the present moment

Definition

A conscious awareness of being present in the moment, noticing and paying attention to internal and external distractions and what is happening, without trying to change things; a conscious non-judgemental acceptance of thoughts, feelings and body sensations.

Signs & symptoms

Living in the now, rather than in the past or the future; having a regular spiritual practice of focusing on and accepting the flow of life.

Mindfulness is a meditation practice where we become fully present to ourselves and our current environment. Most of us focus on the past or future, paying little attention to what's happening in the *now*, which means that for much of the time we're not truly present to our experiences. Focusing on the breath and the body and connection to our environment helps us to observe and accept the way things are – for better or worse – without judgement. It can help to relieve stress, anxiety, depression, addictive behaviour, insomnia and other physical ailments. It can also reduce negative feelings like anger and resentment. In this relaxed state, you are aware of the layers and waves of consciousness.

Support & guidance Find somewhere comfortable to sit or lie down, then begin to notice your breathing. Be aware of the rise and fall of each breath, where your body expands and then falls, the feelings within your body, the flow of movement, the flutters within, or any pain or tension. Connect to your environment. Allow your body to be completely supported and relaxed. If you're sitting, connect the soles of your feet to the floor, be aware of the energy inside you and the external temperature on the different parts of your body. Become aware of background noises; name them, without judgement or inquiry. Bring your attention to your mind; notice any specific thoughts that you have or a background of persistent thoughts that bother you. Name the thoughts. Choose to hold them, or release them and let them float away. You are in a zone of mindful peace within.

How do you relax and let go of thinking?
How could mindfulness help you?

UPSET

Definition
—

Feeling unhappy, disappointed, worried, off balance.

Signs & symptoms
—

Crying, confusion, sadness, emptiness, tears; avoidance, withdrawal, separation, anxiety.

Feeling upset usually relates to conflict with others or disappointment in the way we feel we are being treated by them. We are more likely to be affected by people we care about than the behaviour of strangers. When feeling upset it may be hard to think straight, and all kinds of assumptions are made which can feed into our own feelings of self-worth, rejection or abandonment. We may feel disrespected, unloved, uncared for, passed over and ignored. It can also be about regretting our own behaviour. There are times when we don't get it right (we're human, after all), when we're moody, miserable or angry, and might take it out on someone we love, or anyone who happens to be in our way. If we feel vulnerable, we might project our feelings onto others through attack or blame. Self-awareness is key.

Support & guidance When you feel upset or confused, it's always best to try and communicate with the person face-to-face. What we believe in our minds to be the case might not necessarily be so; there are at least two sides to every story. It doesn't mean you are at fault but it might help you understand. Are you being too giving? Have you put strong boundaries around yourself? What can you do in future? We usually know in the back of our minds when we do wrong, but to admit it is another thing entirely. It's easier to carry on regardless or ignore our own or others' feelings. 'Sorry' goes a long way, but not everyone finds it easy to say. An apology shows strength, and that a person is willing to be accountable. Remember: things are never quite as bad as they seem at the time.

What upsets you most in life?
How do you help yourself to feel better?

ENLIGHTENED

Definition

Seeing the light; the reality of self and others. Expanded consciousness taking you above subjective experience; being rational and informed.

Signs & symptoms

Inner wisdom; open-minded; open-hearted. Being on a spiritual journey; belief that whatever happens is meant to be.

Enlightenment is a subjective experience of awareness and awakened energy. It's about truth and clarity, having your eyes open to reality or having knowledge and understanding that throws light onto darkness or confusion – an internal wisdom that requires no justification or explanation. It's that 'lightbulb' moment when everything makes sense and fits into place. It strips away illusions, masks and rose-coloured spectacles – bears witness to self and others, and allows for continual growth and learning. To be enlightened is to be knowing, and accepting of what life offers without resistance or unnecessary expectation, disappointment or attachment to outcome. Alternatively, it can drive change for progress, fairness and equality.

Support & guidance Start by accepting yourself for who you are, taking off any cloaks of tension or fear. Live fully, with passion and intensity. Love freely and purely without expectation of love in return. Be grateful for small things. Find your true life purpose – what you are here for. When your passion crosses with your actions, you are on your true spiritual path. Practise the art of non-reaction; observe yourself observing life. Feel peace and harmony within yourself and with others. Nobody is truly alone in this world – the energy that flows through you flows beyond you: there is a universal light/life-force holding and supporting you on your journey. Move yourself out of the collective grid of self-interest and into a place of openness. Meditate to quieten your mind and expand your mental focus and awareness. The light is within you!

How could being more enlightened serve you?
What do you need to let go of?

That wonderful feeling when something out of the blue happens

SURPRISE

Definition

A feeling of mild astonishment or shock caused by something unexpected.

Signs & symptoms

Excitement; feeling speechless or breathless; disbelief.

Life can sometimes be very predictable, even boring, when suddenly something happens out of the blue. Surprises can be positive, negative or both. Unexpected news, such as winning the lottery, might even leave you dumbfounded … as might a surprise birthday party that you had no idea about, standing in the middle of a room surrounded by friends and family, feeling grateful and blessed, listening to people saying wonderful things about you, feeling blown away and perhaps a little shaken at the same time. Surprises are moving experiences, mentally, physically and spiritually. An unpleasant surprise might connect to other people's unexpected negative behaviour towards you, or to circumstances such as redundancy or a relationship ending – either can leave you feeling bewildered and floored.

Support & guidance Because surprises are unexpected, we can't plan for them and have no choice but to go with them. If the surprise isn't positive, it may take you a while to process it before you can move on. Try to talk to friends or family if this is upsetting you. We can't be in control of external factors or other people's behaviour. Being surprised or shaken up takes you out of your comfort zone and can leave you feeling discombobulated. When a surprise is a positive, happy experience, like a trip to New York or finding out that you're pregnant, savour each and every moment of the journey. Or, perhaps you have surprised yourself with your own success? Maybe you could enjoy planning a lovely surprise for someone you care about.

Do you like surprises or do you prefer to know what's happening?
When was the last time you had a good surprise? Did it change things for you?

I'm full of energy, passion and anticipation for great things.

EXCITED

Definition

Stirred up with enthusiasm, keenness and passion.

Signs & symptoms

Imagination firing on all cylinders; high energy; wanting to jump from the rooftops – or at least up and down.

Excitement is generated when something really positive happens out of the blue, like winning a prize or being spontaneous and buying two cute little kittens – or looking forward to a planned life event like getting married, moving to a new home or having a baby. We imagine all the joy these types of occasions can bring and see all kinds of happy scenarios way into the future. When you fully embrace the future, it becomes the present and the fun starts. Excitement is also linked to enthusiasm, motivation, intuition and fear; anticipation is never boring. New opportunities and relationships bring excitement and hope. Sometimes you may even have to rein in your excitement to keep yourself grounded.

Support & guidance Excitement is good for the soul. Are you an excitable person or more calm and nonchalant? Sometimes life can feel boring and mundane, so it's important to have things to look forward to, but also to be spontaneous. Do you have enough excitement in your life? What do you feel passionate about? Perhaps booking a holiday or working towards something. When was the last time you did something out of the blue – something random and really challenging? Now and again it's good to step out of our comfort zone, take up new hobbies, travel to new destinations, meet new people and find different ways to experience joy and fun. If you want life to be more exciting, hang out with exciting people! Say yes to opportunities, seek out the weird and wonderful and stay tuned to the inspiration channel.

Who or what excites you?
What can you do to bring more excitement into your life?

BULLIED

Definition

Being targeted (physically or emotionally), intimidated, manipulated, put down, patronized, excluded, blamed, made to feel guilty.

Signs & symptoms

Feeling vulnerable, anxious, stressed, confused; hiding – missing school or work.

Bullying can either be subtle or obvious, and is intended to make another person feel weak or vulnerable, in order to prop up the bully's self-esteem. The underlying desire is to control, dominate, subjugate and eliminate, with little regard or concern for the rights, needs and feelings of others. Being bullied is a damaging experience with long-term effects, and needs to be taken very seriously. It happens in playgrounds but also in the workplace, and sadly this is often ignored. People who are highly sensitive, excel at what they do, are kind, caring and popular, often become targets for bullies, who want to steal their shine.

Support & guidance Being bullied can lead to stress and depression if left to continue. It may feel like you're alone and nobody will believe you, or you can't speak out because the behaviours only happen when nobody else is there, or they're so subtle that others don't notice. You may not even recognize what is happening, because bullying creeps up on you. You're probably hoping it will go away, or even blaming yourself in some way. Your instinct doesn't lie. If you're feeling uncomfortable in the presence of another, or picking up on negative energy or feeling drained by someone, or their comments feel like a stab to the soul, listen to what your body is telling you. It's not OK to bully. In a work situation, report it – keep a diary and let your voice be heard. However, don't be surprised if you don't get the response you would like. Sometimes walking away will be the best decision you ever make. Bullying is toxic – would you drink from the poisoned cup?

Have you ever experienced bullying?
How do you protect yourself from bullies?

I feel a wave of enthusiasm for my achievements.

PROUD

Definition

Feeling deep pleasure or satisfaction as a result of your own achievements, qualities, possessions; pride in someone you care about.

Signs & symptoms

Beaming with pride, singing your praises or those of others; a quiet humble feeling of satisfaction at your own performance.

We experience pride when we know we've worked hard and can finally sit back and feel good about ourselves and our achievements. Why not sing your own praises if you've done well? Pride comes from having confidence in who you are and a strong sense of self. How much you talk about your success can also depend on culture and how acceptable it is to do so. Talking with pride about what you've achieved can be a great inspiration to others. We can also feel pride in others and their achievements, big or small. There's nothing quite as powerful as that sense of pride that a parent experiences when their child takes their first steps, wins a race at school or graduates from college. When our children do well, we can be proud too. We've played a key part in their progress.

Support & guidance Some people find it hard to be proud, because they're always pushing for the next goal and don't take the time to sit back and enjoy the moment. Others find it hard to be proud of themselves, because of low self-esteem and negative thinking. Pride is a measure of your self-worth. It's not being vain or showing off. If you struggle to feel pride, look kindly towards yourself and recognize your strengths, your skills and your personal qualities. What differences have they made to your life so far and those around you? How would your best friend describe you? Hold your head high, enjoy your achievements and fly your flag of pride.

What has been your proudest moment?
Do you find it easy or hard to sing your own praises?

I know what I did was wrong and I'm sorry.

SORRY

Definition

Feeling regret or remorse; being sad or troubled about something; feeling compassion for someone.

Signs & symptoms

Distress, sorrow, regret; feeling guilty, apologetic, concerned, empathetic.

Do you find it hard to say sorry? Or do you wait longingly to hear that word? The power of an apology can make a huge difference in a relationship. There are times when we don't get it right, are moody, miserable or angry, and we might take it out on someone we love, or anyone who happens to be in our way. If we feel vulnerable, we might attack other people or blame them unnecessarily. These actions are unfair and can be hurtful to others. We usually know, in the back of our mind, that what we did was wrong; to admit it is another thing entirely. It's easier to carry on regardless or ignore the consequences. If you have a conscience and clear morals, you'll be able to apologize if you get something wrong.

Support & guidance The ability to reflect on our behaviours shows we're self-aware and have room for personal growth – being able to apologize is a strength. But if you don't feel sorry, don't just say it to please another. It's always best to be honest. It's also important to listen to others and find out how they feel about the situation. This is how relationships grow and deepen into more long-lasting connections. We all make mistakes; it helps us to grow on our spiritual path. Being sorry shows that you're conscious of who you are and how you want to be. Are you willing to look at yourself and take responsibility for your actions? It means a lot to know that someone regrets what they've done, can see the impact of their actions and is remorseful. If you're feeling hurt by the actions of another, it can feel confusing and upsetting, and you may begin to question yourself. Communicate!

How do you feel when you get things wrong?
Is it easy or difficult to say sorry? What stops you?

SOMETHING BAD
MIGHT HAPPEN

FEAR

Definition

*A response to imminent danger or
an anxious feeling caused by a perceived
threat of something bad, challenging
or harmful.*

Signs & symptoms

*Feeling anxious and stressed, having
panic attacks, avoiding activities
or situations.*

Fear can be rational or irrational. When faced with danger, it's a natural inbuilt response and reaction: the survival instinct. Irrational fear ties in with worry, stress and anxiety that stems from negative thinking about the past or the future. You might expect something bad to happen because of a perceived wrongdoing or judgement on you. It's 'worst-case scenario' thinking. We fear what is outside our control or comfort zone. For example, when starting a new job: 'Will they like me?' 'Can I do it?' Fearful thoughts can quickly spiral out of control. A phobia is a more specific fear, such as fear of flying, snakes, heights, spiders, contamination or danger, and often results in avoidance of activities or OCD.

Support & guidance When you have a genuine reason to be afraid, take all steps to protect and defend yourself. You are worth it! If your fear comes from your own anxieties or insecurity, however, take charge of your thinking by recognizing when you are heading into a spiral of negativity. A fearful thought has powerful negative energy and unnecessary consequences. CBT can help to retrain/programme your mind so your thoughts are helpful and work *for* you, rather than *against* you. And hypnotherapy can be a powerful way to combat phobias. Don't suffer alone – there is plenty of professional support out there to help you manage your fears. Stand up to your fear by harnessing the power within you.

What is your biggest fear?
How can you overcome it?

PARANOID

Definition

Irrational thoughts and feelings that someone or something is out to get you; can be a mental disorder.

Signs & symptoms

Being delusional and distrusting; isolating and avoiding others due to fear and anxiety.

Now and again, we all feel uncertain or mistrusting of others, but when your thoughts are relentless and get in the way of everyday life with no valid reason, then perhaps your mind is playing delusional paranoid games with you. You might think you're being watched, talked about, followed, excluded, made to look bad or even at risk of serious physical harm. You may be overly suspicious – looking for clues and double meanings, investigating noises or changes in your environment, interrogating and questioning others – or generally feel like you're on high alert. Paranoid thoughts, although irrational, are believed to be true, so responses to protect and defend are appropriate to the belief.

Support & guidance Those prone to paranoid thinking have trouble trusting others, doubt loyalty, look for hidden motives and are hypersensitive to criticism. They're quick to become hostile and are defensive and argumentative, which leads to social isolation and detachment. If this sounds like you, take control. Try keeping a diary and recording your thoughts, how you feel about them and how they affect you. Look at the triggers and your responses. To help you make sense of it all, ask yourself questions: 'Would others think my suspicions are correct?' 'What is the evidence to support my belief?' 'What are the other possibilities?' If your thoughts are obsessional, try focusing on other activities like exercise, walking or listening to music. Share your worries with friends to lighten the load. This will reduce your anxiety and may bring clarity. If you can't shake the paranoia, seek professional help.

What makes you paranoid?
How do you control your thinking?

I am calm, relaxed and accepting of all that is. I am at peace.

PEACE

Definition

A calm internal state of mind and body, where energy flows without tension or obstacles. A period without disturbance; an absence of conflict.

Signs & symptoms

Finding harmony in difficult situations; letting go of control and expectations of yourself and others. Feeling tranquil, and free from tension; a warm feeling.

Peace comes from knowing and accepting our limitations, from taking pressure off ourselves to achieve certain goals, and an awareness and acceptance of what is and isn't possible. Peace is contentment with your life and gratitude for your blessings, not yearning more or feeling that something is lacking; it's feeling calm and relaxed and taking time to smile, listen and engage with others in a positive way. Peace is ignoring trouble, walking away from arguments, not taking things personally, holding your head high and believing in yourself. External peace, however, isn't within our control. Living in conflict or a war zone makes it very hard to feel peace, but it can be found within us all, even at the worst of times.

Support & guidance To bring more peace into your life, think about what plays on your mind and stops you feeling calm. Are you dwelling on the past or the future? What has gone is over, so let it go; the future is yet to come. Let go of resentments and anger, which won't hurt others but only spoil your peace. Mindfulness, a conscious awareness of the present moment, can help you to find inner calm. Our minds and bodies are entwined, so be aware of the language you use. Make your thoughts peaceful – 'I feel calm', 'I feel relaxed'. Every day brings new opportunities to practise peace. The world will go on around you, but you don't have to engage in the dramas. Being detached doesn't mean you don't care. Compassion from a place of peace will bring a quiet wisdom to any situation. Align your actions with your purpose for peace and contentment.

What does peace mean to you?
What brings you peace?

Case studies

CASE STUDY: *Relationship issues*

Ava, a 35-year-old creative designer for an advertising agency, came to see me because she was having relationship issues. Dreadfully unhappy and feeling anxious, she was desperate to find Mr Right and settle down and have children. She had been seeing her partner, Max, for four years, but the relationship was not feeling good or heading in a positive direction. They weren't living together, and he regularly let her down, making excuses and cheating on her. He would also tell her the relationship was over, but then send her texts asking to be friends. Ava kept going back to him, and would then feel ashamed and judged. The relationship was affecting her mental health, and her self-esteem was on the floor.

We worked with the following moods and emotions over a number of sessions, to help her make sense of herself and the situation.

REJECTED

Rejection is a thread that has run through Ava's life. Her father left her mother when she was three, and she rarely saw him. He then went on to have other children with his new partner, and there was no space for her in his home or his life. She feels worthless as a person. Talking about rejection enabled her to identify the links in the way she views men. By asking 'What can you learn from this?' it helped her to understand that it doesn't always have to be this way. She needs to love herself, not reject herself. She also needs to recognize patterns that cause her to feel bad about herself, and then act on them.

Because her feelings were so conflicted, we then explored the confusion within her to try to make sense of things.

CONFUSED

Ava was confused about the mixed messages from Max. We talked about the communication between them, and whether he knows what type of relationship she is looking for. She has told him a couple of times she wants to settle down with him, and they even started looking at properties together online. This caused her to build up her hopes. She has been saving hard for their future, but he is not doing the same. When I asked the question 'What do you think it all means?' she reluctantly and tearfully admitted to herself that he is not committed to a future with her. The question enabled her to find clarity and be honest with herself.

Ava then got very upset, so we talked about how hurt she feels and the pain of this relationship.

HURT

She can't believe he treats her this way, and the hurt runs deep. She said she tries to be the best girlfriend she can be, so we talked about whether she tries too hard, and she admitted she is always trying to please him so that he will love her. She feels out of control, and is always waiting for cues from him. Her happiness depends on his love for her, but right now she will just settle for having him back. She can't give up on him. Exploring the advice in the book enabled her to get to the root of her problem – her fear of being abandoned and alone. She talked about falling apart without him, which was scary for her.

I was interested to know what it was about this man and this relationship that felt so powerful and intense, and Ava said she felt an attachment to him.

ATTACHMENT

I asked her what Max meant to her, and why she felt she couldn't let him go. She said he was her soulmate, and that being with him helped her to feel whole, so I asked, 'How does holding on help?' Ava talked about the hope that she is worth loving. I suggested she give herself affirmations – positive statements to help her feel stronger.

We ended the session by looking at the different ways she valued herself. I wanted her to see that she is valuable and whole, and worthy of love.

VALUED

Ava said she values truth and honesty. I asked her what she values in herself; she said her kindness and sensitivity. These questions gave her a fresh perspective on how her own values are in conflict with the way she allows others to treat her. This helped her to think about moving forward and away from Max.

Other moods and emotions we explored that helped Ava over time were jealousy, resentment, motivation and gratitude.

CASE STUDY: *Stress and anxiety*

Rob is a trainee doctor – and a perfectionist. He struggles with high workload and often feels overwhelmed by his schedule. In addition, he has social anxiety and struggles with friendships and relationships. His life is a strict routine of work, with little time for rest and definitely not a lot of play. He decided to try counselling because he was feeling very stressed and worried that he would fail his final exams. He was finding it hard to sleep, eat and concentrate. Initially, he struggled to communicate in the sessions, especially when it came to his feelings and emotions, and it was hard for me to get a sense of his personality – of who he was. He had very low self-esteem and confidence, and kept making apologies for himself: 'I'm sorry I'm getting upset'; 'I'm sorry, I don't know what's wrong with me'; 'I know I shouldn't feel this way.'

SELF-DOUBT

It emerged that Rob was very unsure of himself, and so felt the need to make excuses for his thoughts and feelings. He feared rejection by others. An awareness of being judged started very early in Rob's life. His parents had very high expectations of him to follow in the family tradition of medicine. His father was a control freak and a bully. However hard Rob worked at school, it was never good enough. His mother was kind to him but didn't protect him or defend him from his father. In school, at the age of twelve, he was ridiculed by a teacher in front of the class, then bullied by classmates because of it. He learned to defend himself by putting up an emotional barrier that detached him from possible future pain or rejection – it was easier not to make friends. These early experiences affected the way Rob viewed himself, as not being 'good enough', and his assumptions of how others viewed him. He worked hard to gain his place at medical school and it meant everything to him to complete the course.

We then looked at his stress and how it affected him:

STRESS / ANXIETY

Because Rob was unhappy with himself, he found his energy being taken up with unhelpful thoughts, self-criticism and rumination. This was draining him and affecting his ability to work effectively. He had so much in his head that I asked him to make a list of everything that was bothering him. He was quick to write a long list of all his worries. The theme that ran through that list was his lack of confidence in himself and how others perceived him. There was a lot of concern about how to communicate with friends, what he should say or not say, how to be popular and how to keep friendships. He felt lonely and isolated. I asked him to choose a topic to talk about from his list of worries, and he chose to talk about how he feels judged by others.

JUDGED

Rob was his greatest critic. Yes, there had been difficult incidents in his past, but now he had the opportunity for great success. Giving Rob the space to explore his emotions meant he began to find it easier to accept himself – even like himself – and see that he could be a good friend, or even partner.

CONFIDENT / VALUED / ACCEPTANCE

Over the course of the counselling sessions, we worked together at building Rob's confidence and learning to accept and value himself. It was hard for him to trust others, because his life story so far had taught him that people who are supposed to care for you hurt you. His past didn't need to determine his future.

I used a number of techniques and models to help Rob let go of his past, including NLP (neuro-linguistic programming), hypnotherapy and inner-child work. We also worked on changing his mindset using a CBT approach – CBT aims to identify unhelpful or irrational thinking and replace it with more positive thoughts and actions.

I taught Rob about meditation and mindfulness and how to be more present in the moment, and also not to dismiss his difficult thoughts and feelings, but to accept them as a part (not the whole) of himself. Going forward, this helped him to relax (see overleaf).

RELAXED / MEDITATIVE

Rob knew something had to give – he wanted a better work/life balance, with time for fun and relaxation. He let go of his fear about socializing and joined group activities like theatre trips and walking weekends.

Rob has since qualified and works in the local hospital. I see him riding his bike to work and I sense that he has now found his inner peace and contentment.

CASE STUDY: *Eating disorder*

Emma is 13 and has anorexia and body dysmorphic disorder. In addition to counselling, she also attends an eating disorder unit to help her to increase her weight. Emma doesn't want to put on weight and feels angry when she's told that she's making improvements. Together, we tried to uncover the causes of the problem; a number of issues are emerging, such as her struggles with schoolwork and how she compares herself to her friends.

We worked with the following moods and emotions over a number of sessions, to try and shed some light on the underlying factors.

NEGATIVE

First of all, we worked with Emma's feelings of negativity. She was aware that she has probably always been a negative person: 'I'm the one who always sees what will go wrong in the family.' When I asked Emma how her negative thinking affects her, she told me that it stops her from doing things because she doubts they'll go well, so she doesn't see the point. Some of her typical negative thoughts include things like: 'I'm not good enough'; 'It won't work'; 'That's not right'; 'It won't be good'; 'I might as well give up.'

When I asked her about the positive things she could say about herself, or what she likes about herself, she really struggled to answer and was only able to say that she liked her friends and she liked sport. I prompted her to find something she was good at, so that there was at least one thing on the list. It was obvious from her answers, and from further conversation, that she has very low self-esteem and finds it hard to see anything good in herself. We talked about how negative her thinking is, and that if she was able to change her thoughts, this might help her to feel better. (I was using a CBT approach.) A thought is just the message you give yourself – which you can choose. She liked the idea that she could control her thoughts and even came up with an affirmation, which was a step in the right direction: '*I can choose positive thoughts.*' Emma said that she wants to feel stronger, because she wants to beat the eating disorder.

I wanted her to learn to connect to her power and her strength, so together we looked at what it meant to be strong and what that might feel like.

STRONG

I asked Emma where she gets her strength from. She told me she just wants to be normal, like her friends. I asked her how she shows her strength, and she told me: 'Every day I have to hide my feelings, so I put on a mask with a smile, but inside I feel like I'm breaking up. I don't want my friends to see me weak; I don't want them to know. They think I'm OK, but I'm not.' This young girl was so strong inside; it made me realize how hard it was for her to hold in all her feelings. There was a moment of strong empathy and connection between us, and I knew that she knew I understood how hard this experience is for her and what a brave girl she is to keep going, turning up at school, trying her hardest. She said that being strong helps her to keep going.

We then went back to the list of positive things she could say about herself and she was quite easily able to add: '*I can be strong.*' This made her smile and I could see that her energy had completely changed.

The next time Emma came to counselling, we looked at her anxieties, worries and fears.

ANXIETY / WORRIED / FEAR

Emma's biggest fear was failure – of not passing exams, not being able to study properly or go to university. She described herself as being stupid. She also told me she has other rituals to influence outcomes, such as counting steps on the way to school and placing items in certain ways. She had strong thoughts and beliefs about what would happen if she failed to perform these tasks.

Emma was very unhappy, but didn't know how to change things. It transpired that she had been a worrier from a very young age and wanted to be a 'good girl' and get things right. She put a lot of pressure on herself to please her parents and teachers, but this had now become overwhelming and unrealistic. Using a CBT approach, we looked together at her irrational and unhelpful thoughts and her belief in them. She had a very black-and-white view of life, so my aim was to help her see the grey areas and become more flexible and accepting of herself.

RELIEF

After several sessions and lots of practice, Emma said that she felt relief about herself and her situation. She had put on weight and no longer focused on her body image: 'I can breathe again. I've let go of thinking of food – it's a huge weight off my shoulders.' She had more self-acceptance and was OK with the thought that she might get things wrong or make mistakes sometimes. The pressure was off.

CASE STUDY: *Relationship with a narcissistic mother*

Sara (48) came to see me to gain more understanding about the toxic relationship she has with her mother. She had recently been reading a lot about narcissists and felt stupid that it had taken her so long to identify the problem and to recognize her mother's behaviours (over many years) falling into toxic patterns of manipulation. Sara could also recognize some of these characteristics in herself, which made it hard to bear. Unsurprisingly, she had co-dependency issues and was married to a narcissist.

We looked at the impacts of narcissism, the behaviours and coping strategies.

NARCISSIST

Sara's mother was only really interested in herself. Although she asked Sara questions about her life, Sara rarely felt listened to. Communication felt more like an interrogation. This often left her feeling sad and disappointed. Mother could never be wrong, even when her behaviour flouted all boundaries and respect for her daughter. If challenged, even at the smallest level, this would lead to a barrage of self-pitying, angry, vitriolic accusations, followed by tears and blame and a recollection of everything Sara had ever done wrong and all that her mother had ever done right. Her mother was self-righteous, with little self-awareness, poor empathy and a lack of ability to take personal responsibility when things went wrong between them. In addition, her mother managed to manipulate other members of the family, using Sara as a scapegoat – the problem daughter.

Sara had poor coping strategies when things went wrong, feeling confused and like a child being told off when it's not their fault. A lot of the time, Sara just cried. She also blamed her mother and found it hard to recognize her own part in these dramas. There were similarities between them, which really bothered her.

The next emotion we looked at in depth was guilt.

GUILT

Guilt was what Sara was left with after an incident. What would her mother think of her? Would she be rejected? Was it her fault? What must she do to win back her mother's love? She told me her mother seemed to have a way of making her feel guilty, like she was the bad/ naughty/rude/disobedient one. Did she deserve to be punished and cast aside? Should she apologize?

Most times, Sara didn't feel like saying sorry at all. She was angry, but there was no point in expressing it. She could never win, be right or hope to be heard. If she spoke about her feelings, they would be trampled on.

Sara recognized herself as being extremely passive-aggressive, so we looked at her own reactions and behaviours. It's very easy to lose sight of yourself when caught in the chaos of another person's toxic drama.

PASSIVE-AGGRESSIVE

Sara would play 'nicey-nicey' to her mother, pretend she was fine, but underneath she would be angry and upset. The problem was that, when she held onto the anger, it was her that suffered — and the wedge between them grew bigger and bigger. What she wanted to say to her mother was: 'You are a selfish woman. You can never do wrong, can you? You can't take responsibility or own up to your part in things. You can never see it from my point of view, you don't care about me, I'm nothing to you.' Instead, she stayed quiet, behind a smiling mask. She was confused and desperately wished things were different between them.

As time went on, we looked at many other emotions in the therapy room:

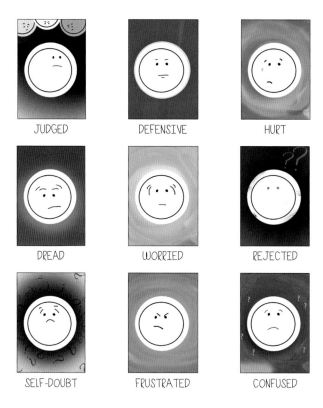

How Sara felt judged by her mother – there was no unconditional love.

How Sara felt defensive around her mother – she had to protect herself from being hurt and couldn't be open and honest.

How Sara felt dread at the thought of seeing her mother or speaking to her – it was always just a matter of time before the next incident.

How Sara worried about rejection by her mother, even though she wanted to be the one to reject. She couldn't let go – it was her mother, after all.

How Sara had long periods of self-doubt, frustration and confusion, trying to make sense of situations and unravelling conversations and ruminating on them.

A lot of the work we did together focused on empowering Sara to build strength and set clear boundaries around herself. We worked on being assertive, so she could stand up to her mother as an equal adult, rather than a regressed child.

ASSERTIVE

Sara recognized that she could be very assertive when it came to her own children. There was nothing she wouldn't do to protect them. I asked her if she could do the same for herself, to see that small child inside her who needed protecting and loving, to see that she's an equal to her mother and no longer has to 'do as she's told'. I explained that it's OK for Sara to have her own opinions and feelings, and it's also OK to express them, in a non-threatening way: 'I felt upset by your response to me the other day.' 'It hurts my feelings when you do X, so I would appreciate it if you could please stop.'

We can't control how others perceive us, respond to us or judge us. What we can control is being the best version of ourselves, standing up for ourselves, not allowing another person to control us, dominate us or diminish us.

Narcissism takes some standing up to, and Sara is on the journey of understanding and self-awareness.

A–Z directory

Connect with Andrea

To find out more about me and the way I work, please take a look at my websites, where I have well over 100 articles on a variety of topics:

www.themoodcards.com

www.andreaharrn.co.uk

You can also connect with me on:
• Twitter @themoodcards or @moodcards
• Instagram @themoodcards
• LinkedIn or Facebook at Andrea Harrn Psychotherapist

If you are interested in discovering other ways to work with the moods and emotions explored in this book, why not check out the Mood Cards packs (for more details, please visit www.themoodcards.com).

Acknowledgements

First and foremost, huge gratitude to everyone at Eddison Books for supporting me as an author in so many ways. Thank you Tessa Monina (and team) for your patience and mindful editing skills and Charlotte Gravell for help with social media engagement. Special thanks to Séverine Jeauneau and the sales team for fantastic results in such a short time. You are amazing!!!

Heartfelt thanks to my agent Sandy Violette, at the Abner Stein Agency. I could not have done this without you personally and your extensive industry knowledge and support.

Huge appreciation and gratitude to the incredibly talented and creative illustrator Stacey Siddons, who has been with me from the early conception of *The Mood Cards*. Your support to me is truly valued and I look forward to many more years working together.

Massive love and thanks to Melissa June Hobbs for being such a diligent researcher; you have played a key role in the Mood Card journey and I really appreciate you.

To my husband Andrew, thank you for your love and encouragement, and trying your best to understand me, which I'm sure isn't easy for you as a non-empath, left-brain, logical alpha male!

To my mum Helena Hockley, thank you for teaching me right from wrong, to be a good person, to do the right thing, to think of others and to be the best I can be. I was a wild child but you never gave up on me.

To my dear sister Beverly Feldman, you are the most sincere, beautiful loving sister anyone could wish for. Thank you for always being there when I need someone to talk to.

To my sister Diane, sweet and innocent in your own special way. I guess trying to fix minds started with yours. I didn't manage that one but you can't win them all!

To my children Alex, Victoria and Ben, who I love more than words can say. You continue to inspire me, make me laugh and provide lots of opportunity for fun. I'm so proud of the way you live your lives. To Kerri, Tom, Mathilde, Jon, Talia, Tash and Lee – love you all and feel blessed to have you in our ever-growing family.

To my beautiful adorable little grandsons, Oilibhéar and Theo – may all your dreams come true. To my grandchildren to come, I look forward to meeting you and loving you with all my heart.

Huge thanks and respect to all my clients, past and present. We have learnt so much from each other and I feel blessed to have met you on our life journeys.

I would also like to honour and thank all my dear friends who are there for me when needed. We go back a long way and a short way and I feel blessed to have you in my life. Specifically: Jill Wershof, Linda Freeman, Carol Hobbs, Sandra Forkes, Verna Jaffe, Ruth Giemajner, Toni Rose, Barb Lasher, Roz Crampton, Sandy Daly and Beverly Compton.

Massive thanks to everyone who has left a review on Amazon, and those who connect with me on social media – especially to my Facebook friends and community, who have fully and wholeheartedly engaged in conversation about moods, emotions, life and mental health issues. I love and appreciate each and every one of you.

Lastly, thank you to everyone that has bought this book.

Andrea

EDDISON BOOKS LIMITED
Managing Director Lisa Dyer
Managing Editor Tessa Monina
Copy Editor Katie Golsby
Proofreader Nikky Twyman
Designer Brazzle Atkins
Production Sarah Rooney & Cara Clapham
Sales Director Séverine Jeauneau